Student Success Manual

to accompany

Understanding Human Communication

Student Success Manual

to accompany

Understanding Human Communication
Twelfth Edition

Ronald B. Adler
Santa Barbara City College

George Rodman
Brooklyn College, City University of New York

Athena du Pré
University of West Florida

Prepared by
Dan Rogers

New York   Oxford
Oxford University Press

Oxford University Press is a department of the University of Oxford.
It furthers the University's objective of excellence in research,
scholarship, and education by publishing worldwide.

Oxford New York
Auckland Cape Town Dar es Salaam Hong Kong Karachi
Kuala Lumpur Madrid Melbourne Mexico City Nairobi
New Delhi Shanghai Taipei Toronto

With offices in
Argentina Austria Brazil Chile Czech Republic France Greece
Guatemala Hungary Italy Japan Poland Portugal Singapore
South Korea Switzerland Thailand Turkey Ukraine Vietnam

For titles covered by Section 112 of the US Higher Education
Opportunity Act, please visit www.oup.com/us/he for the
latest information about pricing and alternate formats.

Published by Oxford University Press
198 Madison Avenue, New York, New York 10016
http://www.oup.com

Oxford is a registered trademark of Oxford University Press

ISBN: 978-0-19-933850-4

Contents

ACKNOWLEDGEMENTS

Many thanks go out to the following reviewers:

Kimberly Batty-Herbert, South Florida State College

Bryan Brown, Northern Virginia Community College

Jacki Brucher Moore, Kirkwood Community College

Darin Garard, Santa Barbara City College

Beth Gillis, College of DuPage

Amy Knight, Mississippi State University

Cassandra Johnson, Shorter University

Emily McWorthy, Kirkwood Community College

Tammy O'Donnell, Prince George's Community College

Andrea Pearman, Tidewater Community College

Diane Ryan, Tidewater Community College

Tanika L. Smith, Prince George's Community College

Charlotte Toguchi, Kapi'olani Community College

Sherry Tucker, Community College of Baltimore County

Ann Vogel, University of Wisconsin-Oshkosh

INTRODUCTION

LEARNING STYLES

People learn in different ways. Some understand best by reading (and rereading), while others prefer listening to explanations. Still others get the most insight from hands-on experiences. Knowing your preferred way to take in and learn information can contribute to your college success. You might prefer to see information, to hear information, or to work with information in a hands-on way. In college you won't always be able to choose how information comes to you. Professors require lectures, textbooks, essays, labs, videos, and readings. In this section we'll help you understand your preferred learning style and help you discover ways to approach your studies that will work best for you.

In the next few pages we introduce five learning preferences and provide the opportunity for you to identify your own preference. Then you can put that information to work for you. There are many approaches to learning styles and preferences; here we present one of them, VARK, an acronym for Visual, Aural, Read/Write, and Kinesthetic ways of learning. A fifth category, multimodal, recognizes learners who have two or more strong preferences. No approach is better or worse than others; this is an opportunity to identify your learning preference and use that information to facilitate your college success.

The best way to begin is to identify your learning preference. You can do this by completing the following questionnaire.

The VARK Questionnaire

This questionnaire aims to find out something about your preferences for working with information. You will have a preferred learning style, and one part of that learning style is your preference for the intake and output of ideas and information.

Choose the answer that best explains your preference and circle the letter next to it. Please circle more than one if a single answer does not match your perception. Leave blank any question that does not apply, but try to give an answer for at least ten of the thirteen questions.

When you have completed the questionnaire, use the marking guide to find your score for each of the categories, Visual, Aural, Read/Write, and Kinesthetic. Then, to calculate your preference, use the scoring chart.

1. You are about to give directions to a person who is standing with you. She is staying in a hotel in town and wants to visit your house later. She has a rental car. You would

   a. draw a map on paper.
   b. tell her the directions.
   c. write down the directions (without a map).
   d. collect her from the hotel in your car.

2. You are not sure if a word should be spelled "dependent" or "dependant." You would

    a. look it up in the dictionary.
    b. see the word in your mind and choose by the way it looks.
    c. sound it out in your mind.
    d. write both versions down on paper and choose one.

3. You have just received a copy of your itinerary for a world trip. This is of interest to a friend. You would

    a. phone her immediately and tell her about it.
    b. send her a copy of the printed itinerary.
    c. show her on a map of the world.
    d. share what you plan to do at each place you visit.

4. You are going to cook something as a special treat for your family. You would

    a. cook something familiar without the need for instructions.
    b. thumb through the cookbook looking for ideas from the pictures.
    c. refer to a specific cookbook that has a good recipe.

5. A group of tourists has been assigned to you to find out about wildlife reserves or parks. You would

    a. drive them to a wildlife reserve or park.
    b. show them slides and photographs.
    c. give them pamphlets or a book on wildlife reserves or parks.
    d. give them a talk on wildlife reserves or parks.

6. You are about to purchase a new stereo. Other than price, what would most influence your decision?

    a. the salesperson telling you what you want to know
    b. reading the details about it
    c. playing with the controls and listening to it
    d. it looks really smart and fashionable

7. Recall a time in your life when you learned how to do something like playing a new board game. Try to avoid choosing a very physical skill, like riding a bike. You learned best by means of

    a. visual clues—pictures, diagrams, charts.
    b. written instructions.
    c. listening to somebody explaining it.
    d. doing it or trying it.

8. You have an eye problem. You would prefer the doctor to

    a. tell you what is wrong.
    b. show you a diagram of what is wrong.
    c. use a model to show you what is wrong.

9. You are about to learn to use a new program on a computer. You would

    a. sit down at the keyboard and begin to experiment with the program's features.
    b. read the manual that comes with the program.
    c. telephone a friend and ask questions about it.

10. You are staying in a hotel and have a rental car. You would like to visit friends whose address/location you do not know. You would like them to

    a. draw you a map on paper.
    b. tell you the directions.
    c. write down the directions (without a map).
    d. collect you from the hotel in their car.

11. Apart from the price, what would most influence your decision to buy a particular book?

    a. You have read it before.
    b. A friend talked about it.
    c. You quickly read parts of it.
    d. The way it looks is appealing.

12. A new movie has arrived in town. What would most influence your decision to go (or not go)?

    a. You heard a radio review about it.
    b. You read a review about it.
    c. You saw a preview of it.

13. You prefer a lecturer or teacher who likes to use which teaching tools?

    a. a textbook, handouts, readings
    b. flow diagrams, charts, graphs
    c. field trips, labs, practical sessions
    d. discussion, guest speakers

The VARK Questionnaire—Scoring Chart

Use the following scoring chart to find the VARK category that each of your answers corresponds to. Circle the letters that correspond to your answers. For example, if you answered b and c for question 3, circle R and V in the question 3 row.

Question	**a** category	**b** category	**c** category	**d** category
3	A	R	V	K

Scoring Chart

Question	a category	b category	c category	d category
1	V	A	R	K
2	R	V	A	K
3	A	R	V	K
4	K	V	R	
5	K	V	R	A
6	A	R	K	V
7	V	R	A	K
8	A	V	K	
9	K	R	A	
10	V	A	R	K
11	K	A	R	V
12	A	R	V	
13	R	V	K	A

Calculating Your Scores

Count the number of each of the VARK letters you have circled to get your score for each VARK category.

Total number of **V**s circled =   (Visual score)

Total number of **A**s circled =   (Aural score)

Total number of **R**s circled =   (Read/write score)

Total number of **K**s circled =   (Kinesthetic score)

Calculating Your Preferences

Because you can choose more than one answer for each question, the scoring is complex. It can be likened to a set of four stepping stones across water.

1. Add up your scores: V + A + R + K =   (total)

2. Enter your scores from highest to lowest on the stones in the diagram, with their V, A, R, and K labels.

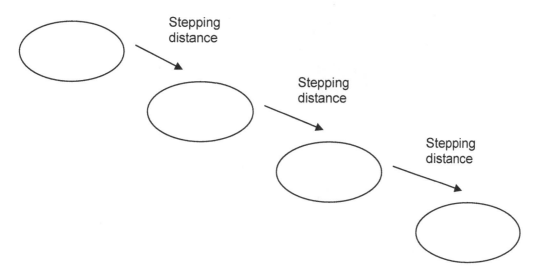

3. Your stepping distance comes from this table.

Total of my four VARK scores is	My stepping distance is
10–16	1
17–22	2
23–26	3
More than 26	4

4. Your first preference is your highest score, so check the first stone as one of your preferences

5. If you can reach the next stone with a step equal to or less than your stepping distance, then check that one too. When you cannot reach the next stone, you have finished defining your set of preferences.

Now that you've scored your questionnaire, find the help sheet in the following pages that matches your preferred learning style. Go to the help sheet for each preference you have checked. If you have more than one preference checked, you should also read the material on multimodal preferences. Look at the specific strategies to study and learn (intake) information during class and independent study and then become familiar with and practice ways that will help you do well on exams (output). Read more about this resource for learning at www.vark-learn.com.

Visual Study Strategies

You want the whole picture, so you are probably holistic rather than reductionist in your approach. You are often swayed by the look of an object. You are interested in color, layout, and design, and you know where you are in your environment. You are probably going to draw something.

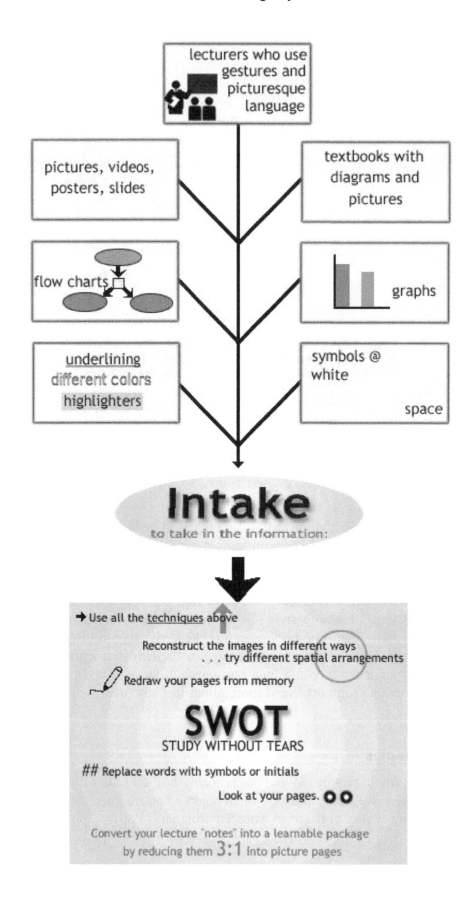

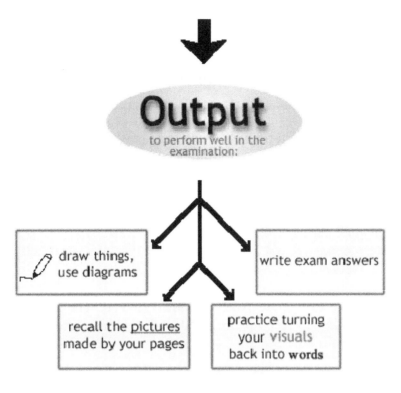

© copyright 2001 Neil Fleming

Aural Study Strategies

If you have a strong preference for learning by aural methods (**A** = hearing), you should use some or all of the following:

> **INTAKE**
> To take in the information:

Attend classes.
Attend discussions and tutorials.
Discuss topics with others.
Discuss topics with your teachers.
Explain new ideas to other people.
Use a tape recorder.
Remember the interesting examples, stories, and jokes.
Describe the overheads, pictures and other visuals to somebody who was not there.
Leave spaces in your notes for later recall and "filling."

> **SWOT—Study without Tears**
> To make a learnable package:

Convert your notes into a learnable package by reducing them (3:1).

- Your notes may be poor because you prefer to listen. You will need to expand your notes by talking with others and collecting notes from the textbook.

- Put your summarized notes onto tapes and listen to them.
- Ask others to "hear" your understanding of a topic.
- Read your summarized notes aloud.
- Explain your notes to another "aural" person.

> ## OUTPUT
> To perform well in any test, assignment,
> or examination:

- Imagine talking with the examiner.
- Listen to your voices and write them down.
- Spend time in quiet places recalling the ideas.
- Practice writing answers to old exam questions.
- Speak your answers aloud or inside your head.

You prefer to have this entire page explained to you. The written words are not as valuable as those you hear. You will probably go and tell somebody about this.

Read/Write Study Strategies

If you have a strong preference for learning by reading and writing, you should use some or all of the following:

> ## INTAKE
> To take in the information:

- lists
- headings
- dictionaries
- glossaries
- definitions
- handouts
- textbooks
- readings—library
- notes (often verbatim)
- teachers who use words well and have lots of information in sentences and notes
- essays
- manuals (computing and laboratory)

> **SWOT—Study without Tears**
> To make a learnable package:

Convert your notes into a learnable package by reducing them (3:1).

- Write out the words again and again.
- Read your notes (silently) again and again.
- Rewrite the ideas and principles into other words.
- Organize any diagrams, graphs, figures, or pictures into statements, for example, "The trend is. . . ."
- Turn reactions, actions, diagrams, charts, and flows into words.
- Imagine your lists arranged in multiple-choice questions and distinguish each from each.

> **OUTPUT**
> To perform well in any test, assignment,
> or examination:

- Write exam answers.
- Practice with multiple-choice questions.
- Write paragraphs, beginnings, and endings.
- Write your lists (a, b, c, d; 1, 2, 3, 4).
- Arrange your words into hierarchies and points.

You like this page because the emphasis is on words and lists. You believe the meanings are within the words, so any talk is okay, but this handout is better. You are heading for the library.

Kinesthetic Study Strategies

If you have a strong kinesthetic preference for learning, you should use some or all of the following:

```
                    INTAKE
           To take in the information:
```

- all your senses—sight, touch, taste, smell, hearing
- laboratories
- field trips
- field tours
- examples of principles
- lecturers who give real-life examples
- applications
- hands-on approaches (computing)
- trial and error
- collections of rock types, plants, shells, grasses, . . .
- exhibits, samples, photographs, . . .
- recipes—solutions to problems, previous exam papers

```
          SWOT—Study without Tears
           To make a learnable package:
```

Convert your notes into a learnable package by reducing them (3:1).

- Your lecture notes may be poor because the topics were not "concrete" or "relevant."
- You will remember the "real" things that happened.
- Put plenty of examples into your summary. Use case studies and applications to help with principles and abstract concepts.
- Talk about your notes with another kinesthetic person.
- Use pictures and photographs that illustrate an idea.
- Go back to the laboratory or your lab manual.
- Recall the experiments, field trips, and so on.

```
                    OUTPUT
        To perform well in any test, assignment,
                  or examination:
```

- Write practice answers and paragraphs.
- Role-play the exam situation in your own room.
  You want to experience the exam so that you can understand it. The ideas on this page are valuable only to the extent that they sound practical, real, and relevant to you. You need to do things to understand.

Multimodal Study Strategies

If you have multiple preferences, you are in the majority, as somewhere between 50 and 70 percent of any population seems to fit into that group.

Multiple preferences are interesting and quite varied. For example, you may have two strong preferences, such as VA or RK, or you may have three strong preferences, such as VAR or ARK. Some people have no particular strong preferences, and their scores are almost even for all four modes. For example, one student had scores of V = 9, A = 9, R = 9, and K = 9. She said that she adapted to the mode being used or requested. If the teacher or supervisor preferred a written mode, she simply used that mode for her responses and for her learning.

So, multiple preferences give you choices of two, three, or four modes to use for your interaction with others. Some people have admitted that if they want to be annoying, they stay in a mode different from the person with whom they are working. For example, they may ask for written evidence in an argument, knowing that the other person much prefers to refer only to oral information. Positive reactions mean that those with multimodal preferences choose to match or align their mode to the significant others around them.

If you have two dominant or equal preferences, please read the study strategies that apply to your two choices. If you have three or four preferences, read the three or four lists that apply. You will need to read two, three, or four lists of strategies. People with multimodal preferences will use more than one strategy for learning and communicating. They feel insecure with only one. Alternatively, those with a single preference often "get it" by using the set of strategies that aligns with their single preference.

There seem to be some differences among those who are multimodal, especially those who have chosen fewer than seventeen options. If you have chosen fewer than seventeen of the options in the questionnaire, you may prefer to see your highest score as your main preference— almost like a single preference. You are probably more decisive than those who have chosen seventeen-plus options.

Summary of VARK Scores

Now that you are familiar with your preferred learning style, come back to these pages and review the activities that will help you learn and process information best. Your favorite learning style may not match the teaching style used by the professor in this course. If that's the case, take the initiative to learn the material in the other ways outlined for you in the preceding pages while you continue to develop your ability to learn in ways that aren't your favored method.

Based on what you learned about your preferred learning method, list five specific things you can do to help yourself learn the material in this communication course.

     1.

     2.

     3.

     4

     5.

STUDY SKILLS

Academic success doesn't just depend on how smart you are or how hard you work: it also depends on how *well* you study. Many students spend hours with their books but don't manage to understand the material they're expected to know. Not all methods of "spending time" with the text are equally productive, so we present here several methods that can help you study effectively.

Use SQ3R

SQ3R is a widely used acronym for an effective method to study a text. The method includes these five steps:

S—Survey
Q—Question
R—Read
R—Recite
R—Review

Survey

Begin by getting an overview of the material you'll later study in detail. Start with one chapter. Look at the title of the chapter and the major headings. Survey the opening page with its Chapter Highlights and objectives. Skim the chapter's tables, photos, cartoons, sidebars, figures, charts, and summaries. Glance at the Critical Thinking Probes and Ethical Challenges. At the end of each chapter, peruse the Key Terms, Activities, and Resources. This big-picture survey will help you put each section of the chapter in a larger context.

Question

Go back over the headings you have just surveyed and turn each one into a question. Most questions will include one of the following words: who, what, when, where, how, or why. Look how topics from *Understanding Human Communication* can fit into these forms:

- Who has power in groups? (Followership and Communication, Chapter 9)
- What are the ways to help others when they have problems? (Supportive Listening, Chapter 5)
- When should you reveal personal information, and when should you keep it to yourself? (Guidelines to Appropriate Self-Disclosure, Chapter 7)
- Where can you find information for your speech? (Gathering Information, Chapter 11)
- How can you paraphrase? (Task-Oriented Listening, Chapter 5)
- Why is misunderstanding so common? (The Language of Misunderstandings, Chapter 4)

Read

Once you've reworded each section as a question, you can read the material to find an answer. Read only one section at a time, to make sure you understand it before going on. As you answer a question, don't just rely on material in the text. Think about what you already know from your life experiences and from other classes.

Consider reading in a way that takes advantage of your strongest learning style. If your learning style is visual, highlight as you read, and translate what you read into pictures, drawings, and diagrams in the margins or in your notes. If your learning style is aural, consider reading the book aloud, taping it, and then listening to the tape. If you learn best by reading/writing, you'll want to read all of the handouts and practice questions provided. If you're a kinesthetic learner, you'll learn by doing the activities on the course website and completing the exercises at the end of each chapter. Review the specific strategies for your learning style presented in the preceding pages and use them.

Recite

After you've read the material, test your understanding by putting the ideas into your own words. Another word for reciting is *explaining*. Your goal here is to test your knowledge by rewording it. You can do this either in writing or by verbally explaining the material to a study partner, friend, or family member.

Reciting takes many forms; in fact, you'd be wise to use as many senses as you can. Consider using the techniques you learned in the VARK analysis. Are there some methods that work particularly well for your learning style? Now is the time to use them. If you're a visual learner, look up from your reading and recite what you've just learned by picturing the answer. Recall a visual from your notes and turn it into words. If you're an aural learner, speak your knowledge aloud and hear it in your own voice. If your preferred learning style is reading/writing, write the answer in your own words and read it in your own handwriting. If you are a kinesthetic learner, try to use all of your senses. Think of real-life experiences and examples of what you're learning; act out concepts by actually practicing the skills in this course in various real situations. Most important in this step is translating information into your own words, not just memorizing someone else's words.

Review

Finally, review what you've learned by creating summarizing statements—either in full sentences or in outlines. You can create review documents in short chunks (e.g., sections of a chapter) or on a chapter-by-chapter basis. These review documents can serve you well as you study for exams, so be sure to save them.

SQ3R is not a method to speed up studying like speed-reading techniques, and it is not a method for cramming the night before a final. It is a long-range approach to better understanding and retaining knowledge learned over the course of the semester. It is a method for studying texts that can help you succeed in this course if applied early and consistently. Learning in small segments and reviewing often results in greater learning and retention than cramming. We have inserted reminders to use this method in each chapter of this *Student Success Manual*.

Additional Study Ideas

Mark Your Texts

Forget the admonitions from your elementary teachers not to mark in your books. Studying is not a passive activity. You want to do more than just read your text; you want to study it, prepare for your exam, and increase your long-term retention of the information. When you mark your text you involve touch and movement, not just vision. This increased activity can stimulate brain activity and aid recall. Writing side notes to yourself, underlining, circling, and highlighting involve you in the process of learning. Here are some guidelines for marking your texts:

1. **Read before you mark.** To be able to figure out what is most important, you need to read a paragraph or section before you mark it up. As you read, try to distinguish main points from details. Analyze as you read to see categories and relationships of ideas. Before you mark, determine what is most important to focus on in order to review and remember.

2. **Develop a code of your own.** You might use circles for thesis statements and underlining for examples. When subpoints are spread out over several pages, you might use one color to highlight items of the same category. Use brackets, parentheses, underlining, or quotation marks; develop a system that works for you. Improve your ability to spot the key ideas, relationships, causes and effects, and contrasts and similarities. If you need to, write down your code at the beginning of the chapter.

3. **Make notes in the margin.** Summarize a section in a few words of your own. Translate information into your way of talking and relate it to the lecture, another class, or your personal life. Create a short outline or drawing in the margin to help you recall or relate information. Annotate for your benefit—do what helps you.

4. **Mark thoughtfully; don't just mark everything.** Marking more than 20 percent of the text defeats the purpose of distinguishing the key information to review later. Read first and think carefully about what to mark.

Choose Your Environment

Choose an effective setting in which to study. A successful study setting has minimal interruptions and distractions from external noise, other people, phones, televisions, and doorbells. Using a computer may help you take notes, organize your information, create study guides, and focus on the material you're learning, or it might distract you with e-mail, instant messages, and the temptation to surf. It will take resolve not to answer the phone or check e-mail during your study time. Think about the physical environment of your study location and its comfort in terms of furnishings, lighting, and temperature. Consider furniture that is comfortable but will not lull you to sleep. Chairs, desks, and lighting should give you space and motivation to read and write. Keep the resources you need (paper, pencils, highlighters, dictionary) but not a lot more. Once you have identified a place that works well for you to study, train yourself to use that place often so your brain associates serious study with that location. College libraries usually have well-designed, well-lit spaces with minimal distractions. The Study Environment Analysis (www.ucc.vt.edu/stdysk/ studydis.html) allows you to analyze study settings to determine the best environment for you.

Attend Study Sessions

If your professor or TA announces a study session, make it a priority to attend. These small sessions provide opportunities to review and ask questions. If your professor does not sponsor study sessions, form a study group with other dedicated students. Talking through the material, reviewing each other's notes, and quizzing each other will enhance your study skills and your comprehension and retention of the course concepts.

Seek Help

Familiarize yourself with your campus tutoring centers and labs, study skills workshops, student success centers, communication labs, supplemental instruction, peer mentoring, learning support services, learning assistance centers, or student learning centers. Check out resources to assist you in studying, writing assignments, and preparing for exams.

If you have a learning difficulty or disability, locate and use available services. The Office of Student Services (or the Office of Special Services) provides screening, diagnosing, and assistance for students with learning difficulties or special needs. If you already have documentation of a special need, take that to the appropriate office to receive services more quickly. If you think you may have dyslexia, attention deficit/hyperactivity disorder (ADHD), or any learning disability, you can arrange for a professional screening. After the screening, you can be referred for further testing or to other services to meet your needs. To those who ask, colleges usually provide note takers, books on tape, additional time for tests, and other reasonable accommodations for special needs.

Taking Notes in Class

The preceding section offered advice for studying on your own. This section will help you understand the material that your professor presents in class. In addition to using the approaches for class lectures, you can use them as a supplement or alternative to the SQ3R approach for better understanding the text and other readings. Two popular methods of note taking are the Cornell format and mind maps.

Cornell Note-Taking System

Taking notes while reading or while listening to a lecture occupies much of your time as a student. One tried-and-true method of note taking is the Cornell system. You can utilize this system with the following steps:

1. Before you begin to take notes, draw a vertical line down the left side of your paper about a fourth of the way over (2 inches from the left on an 8½ × 11 inch page).

2. As you listen for main points (see Chapter 5's section on informational listening), take notes on the right side.

3. Later, as you review your notes, put key words, significant phrases, and sample questions in the left column.

SAMPLE: Cornell Note-Taking System

2. Second, pull out key words and phrases and create questions here.	1. First, take notes on this side. Leave space to add to notes from text or readings. Focus on big ideas.
Group Interdependent What size is a small group?	Groups are collections of individuals that interact over time and are interdependent. Usually between 3 and 20 people.
Hidden agenda	Group members have common goals. Individual goals not shared with the group are called hidden agendas. (One person wants to make connections to get a new job—something just for him—but the group goal is to complete a report.)

Mind Mapping

Mind mapping is a technique you can use to take notes from a lecture or text and improve your recall of the ideas. A mind map is a visual representation of the material that emphasizes relationships of concepts. While an outline emphasizes linear relationships, a mind map (also called a concept map) shows associations, links and connections in a holistic way. An outline is more like a book; a mind map resembles information assembled as Web links. Visual learners especially benefit from this method.

To construct your mind map, follow these guidelines:

1. Start in the middle of a large unlined sheet of paper.

2. Use only key words, not sentences.

3. Use images (arrows, circles, sketches) that help you recall ideas and show relationships between words and groups of words.

4. Use colors to link related ideas and separate others.

5. Be creative.

A mind map of a lecture on listening might look like this:

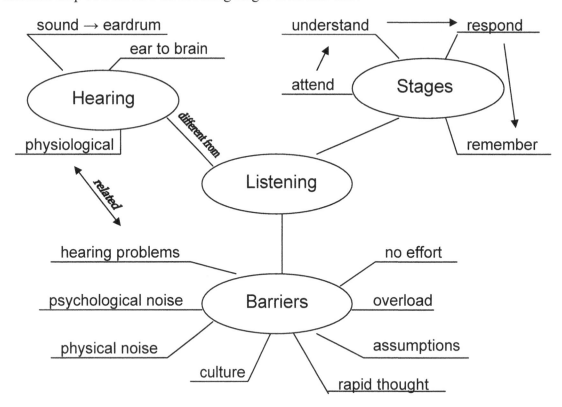

TEST-TAKING SKILLS

In most of your classes, you will take exams. Whether these are short, five-question quizzes or two-hour essay exams, the following tips can help you improve your exam scores.

1. **Prepare for the exam you'll be given.** Read the syllabus carefully or talk with your instructor to find out what types of exams you'll take. Your text, this *Student Success Manual*, and the *Understanding Human Communication* website provide many tools to study for different kinds of exams. Ideally, you'll know the material well enough to be able to pass any type of exam; practically, you can use your time and energy to prepare most efficiently if you know the type of exam you'll be faced with. Here are some pointers for three common types of exam questions.

True/False

A. If the *whole* sentence isn't true, it isn't true. Conversely, if any part is false, it is false. Don't be thrown off by a partial truth buried in an otherwise false statement. Look for any falsehood.

B. Be aware of absolutes (always, never, only) and remember that if there is one exception, the question is false.

C. Statements phrased with negatives can be confusing. If changing it to a positive makes it true, the original sentence phrased as a negative is generally false. For example, "Nonverbal communication cannot be used to deceive." If you make this sentence a positive, it becomes "Nonverbal communication can be used to deceive." Since this is true, the opposite of the sentence must be false.

Multiple Choice

A. Read the first part of the question and think of the answer you would give if no choices were provided. Then see if that is one of the choices.

B. Before marking the answer, read all the choices to be sure yours is the best. Most multiple-choice directions say choose the **best** answer; so all choices may be somewhat correct, but one might be superior to the others. For instance, if you are choosing the best paraphrase, and one choice paraphrases only thoughts and another choice paraphrases only feelings, look for a *best* answer that paraphrases both thoughts and feelings. If one choice is more complete than others, it may be the best choice, even though others may be technically correct, as well.

C. Check if "all (or none) of the above" is a choice. If you know for sure that two or three choices are correct (or incorrect), consider the "all (none) of the above" option.

D. Negative questions can be confusing. If the question is worded as a negative, look at each option and mentally change the question to a positive. Then mark each choice that works. Generally, you will mark all but one, and that one will be the correct answer for the original (negative) question. For example, "Which of the following is **not** a function of nonverbal communication?" can be mentally changed to "Which of these **is** a function of nonverbal communication?" If all but one choice correctly answers the second question, the unmarked question will generally be your answer to the original question.

E. If two choices seem too similar to permit a distinction, reread the question to be sure you understand what is being asked. Check carefully for some small difference in the answers, making one a better choice. Perhaps neither is correct; see if there is a better answer altogether.

Essay

A. Familiarize yourself with the types of words used in essays and be sure you understand their meaning. Commonly used words are *describe, review, explain, compare, contrast, discuss,* and *evaluate*. For each word, the instructor looks for a different reasoning process and type of answer. Read the question carefully and mark the words that tell you what type of answer is expected. Familiarize yourself with the definitions of twenty commonly used words found in essay questions at http://www.studygs.net/essayterms.htm

B. Create an initial outline for each answer. Jot down an outline for each question, organizing your ideas around major themes that answer the question. State your thesis and your support. While you are writing one answer, if an idea pops into your head for another question, quickly add it to the outline.

C. Divide your time so that you will be able to answer each question. Your professor may give you partial credit for an outline or some sentences that show you understand the material, even if the grammar isn't correct and the thoughts aren't complete. Leaving a 10-point question blank results in losing 10 points, no matter how extensive your answer to another question is.

D. Write neatly, leaving space between your lines. This will allow you to go back and add information you think of later. If you are writing and you know the concept but can't think of the precise term or name, leave a blank, describe it, and fill the blank in later. You may think of the term or name as you proceed, or it may be used in another part of the exam.

2. **Predict and prepare for likely types of test questions.** Use the outline provided in this *Student Success Manual* and the more extensive one in the *Study Guide* on the course website to predict objective questions. For instance, if there are four steps or three characteristics listed, be prepared for a multiple-choice question that asks, "Which one of these is . . ." or "Which one of these is not. . . ." Creating an outline or mind map from your lecture notes will help you predict questions on that material.

3. **Use practice questions effectively**. Use the course website to practice multiple-choice, true/false, fill-in-the-blank, and matching questions. Use this *Student Success Manual* to study for short-answer and synthesis questions. When you use sample questions with an answer key, don't look at the answer key while answering the questions. If you simply tell yourself (after seeing the correct answer), "Yes, that's the answer I would have chosen," using the sample exams will not benefit you. Take the sample exams as actual exams without looking at the answers. Then go back and grade yourself. Doing this will reveal gaps in your knowledge and help redirect your study time more productively.

4. **Arrive rested, early, and relaxed**. Be sure you've slept and eaten. Be comfortable and settled before the exam is handed out, with any necessary pens, pencils, and blue books at hand. Put away any unnecessary items so you're not distracted. If you can, relax your body by taking a few slow, deep breaths. Anxiety produces a body on "alert" that is not as capable of test taking as a calmer body.

5. **Plan your time.** Know how much each section of the exam is worth and then set up a time frame for yourself so you'll be able to spend the appropriate amount of time on each section. Check your time to be sure you're staying on task. If there is no penalty for guessing, then guess.

6. **Begin with what you know**. Peruse the exam and jot down ideas for questions you'll answer later. Then begin with the easy questions first to build confidence and get in the swing of things.

7. **Use the hints the exam provides.** Read carefully. Often the answer to one question is contained in another question. Stay alert to information that might be given. If one question is "List and describe the twelve major categories of Jack Gibb's theory of supportive and defensive communication" and another question is "Jack Gibb is best known for his theory of _____," the answer to the second is contained in the first.

8. **Analyze your exam to prepare for the next one.** Always learn from one exam so you can improve on the next one. An exam analysis is provided on the next page. Complete the exam analysis before you talk with your instructor and take it with you; it shows that you are serious about learning from exams, not just grubbing for points.

Postexam Analysis

After your exam, go through the exam and note the number of each item you missed, the code for the type of question you missed, the code for the reason you missed it, and any additional information that is important.

Come up with a plan to improve your studying and your exam scores.

Code for types of questions missed:		
MC = Multiple Choice	**T/F** = True, False	**SA** = Short Answer
E = Essay	**FB** = Fill in the Blank	**M** = Matching

Code for reasons I missed items:

AB = Absent the day it was covered.

NN = Not in my notes, although I was in class and took notes when the item was explained.

N = It was in my notes, but I didn't study or comprehend it.

T = Answer was in the text; I didn't read it or didn't remember it.

MRQ = I misread the question. (reading error)

MUQ = I read the question but misunderstood what was asked. (comprehension error)

V = I didn't understand some of the general vocabulary used to ask the question.

DRC = I didn't read all choices; I picked one I thought was right without reading all.

H = I hurried to get to the end.

RCW = I had it right, erased it, and changed it to a wrong answer.

# Exam question missed	Code for type of question	Code for reason I missed the question	Additional, important information about the question or answer

Now go through your columns and see if you can determine a pattern. Did you miss mostly one type of question? Seek help for answering that type of question. Did you miss questions for one particular reason? What can you do to rectify that?

Write a paragraph in which you summarize what you learn from this analysis and create, in list or paragraph format, a plan to improve the skills you need to do better on the next exam.

WRITING

In addition to study and test-taking skills, your grades in college often hinge on your writing assignments. You've been learning to write for years, and in college it is especially important to apply all you've learned. Successful writing depends on your planning, development, organization, avoidance of plagiarism, and mastery of writing mechanics.

Planning

Read the assignment carefully and ask about anything you don't understand. Underline words on the assignment sheet that give requirements or planning details. Know how long the paper is supposed to be. Begin by clarifying your purpose so you know exactly why you are writing and who your audience is. Understand whether you are being asked to express an opinion, prove a point, analyze a situation, synthesize research, apply a theory, summarize an article, or accomplish some other purpose. Personal response or application papers are very different from book summaries, abstracts, or research papers. Determine whether your paper will be read only by your professor, by a panel, or by classmates as well. If you know your purpose and your audience at the outset, you can plan more successfully. Write down your audience and purpose, and then sketch out a tentative thesis, outline, and possible supporting materials. See the step-by-step advice for planning major papers in "Timeline for a Term Paper" at the end of this section.

Development

Short opinion or analysis papers may not require outside research. They will, however, require that you develop your thoughts and support for your ideas carefully, but not necessarily with outside research. You will improve your development of any paper if you clarify your understanding of the types, functions, and styles of support explained in Chapter 12 of *Understanding Human Communication* ("Supporting Material"). While the activities of writing and speaking differ, the underlying principles and guidelines will serve you well in developing the types of support most appropriate to your paper. Whether you need to check a few facts or conduct extensive research, "Gathering Information" in Chapter 11 will help you develop your paper by using search engines, evaluating websites, and conducting library research.

Organization

Whether preparing papers or speeches, you'll do well to follow the guidelines for organization presented in Chapter 12 of *Understanding Human Communication*. Start with a thesis statement and carefully organize your main points and subpoints in a logical pattern. (See "Principles of Outlining" and "Organizing Your Points in a Logical Pattern.") Then structure your supporting material coherently for greatest impact. Use transitions in your paper as you would in a speech, to help readers understand the direction of your paper and how what you've already said relates to what comes next. (See "Using Transitions.") Finally, when your paper is largely written and you see your creation as a whole, it is time to write an introductory paragraph that gets the readers' attention, states the thesis, and previews the main points. Then write your conclusion so it reviews your thesis and main points and creates closure. Looking at the introduction and conclusion side by side helps you see whether your paper has unity and cohesion. (See "Beginning and Ending the Speech.")

Plagiarism

Virtually every student knows that cheating is a grave academic offense. Nobody who copies answers from a stolen test or a friend can claim ignorance of the rules as a defense. Plagiarism, though, isn't as well understood. Read your college's code of conduct or code of academic integrity to see its definition of academic dishonesty and plagiarism. Here is a breakdown of the most widely recognized types of plagiarism.

Copying

Replicating another person's work word for word is plagiarism. This includes any format or activity that involves taking someone else's work (e.g., a paper, speech, cartoon, or exam) and presenting it as your own in any form (report, speech, or paper). If you are quoting someone else directly in writing, indicate the person's words in quotation marks and properly cite the source. A handbook of English usage will show you how to do citations. In speaking, use an oral citation to clarify the words and the source. Sometimes, plagiarism results from hurried or careless research. If you later cannot determine whether your note cards contain a summary in your own words or quotations from your source, your work may contain plagiarism. Avoid this risk by consistently using quotation marks appropriately and carefully coding your notes.

Paraphrasing

Even if you put others' writings in your own words, you must credit the source. If the words are largely your own paraphrase, but include key words and phrases from another source, put the key words and phrases in quotation marks and cite the source.

Using Ideas

Even though you are not quoting or paraphrasing, credit the source of an idea. The exception is information that is common knowledge and is found without credits in multiple sources of high quality. For instance, almost all communication texts list many types of nonverbal communication, including a category about how far or close we are when we interact with each other. The existence of this category, called proxemics, is common knowledge and needs no citations. However, if you describe the distances at which we interact as "intimate, personal, social, and public," those are the words and ideas of Edward T. Hall, and his work would need to be cited.[1]

---

[1] E. Hall, *The Hidden Dimension* (Garden City, NY: Anchor Books, 1969).

Drawing on Nonprint Sources

The basis of your writing might be a movie, television show, radio broadcast, or website. If ideas, paraphrases, or quotations come from these, be sure to cite them. Style guides and English usage handbooks give you formats for doing so.

In brief, credit those who shape your research and ideas. In the process, your citations demonstrate that you've researched and studied beyond your text. You get credit for researching and also enhance your credibility when you cite quality work. Be sure to do your own synthesizing, analyzing, and reflecting on your research so that your thesis and writing reflect your own thinking and your paper is not just a series of quotations strung together. The ideas, organization, and particular process of asking and answering a research question should be yours. Demonstrate that you have original thoughts, interpretations, analyses, and means of expression supported by current research and experts.

Grammar and Mechanics

No matter how brilliant your thoughts are, grammatical and mechanical errors create "noise" for the grader, causing your ideas to get lost. Use complete sentences to create coherent paragraphs. A spelling and grammar check on your computer helps, but it misses errors of many types, so don't rely solely on it. Use the online and in-person resources available to you to review grammar and spelling concerns. After you proofread, have a tutor or competent friend read your paper to see if it makes sense, is readable, and is free of errors. Double-check that your paper adheres to specific requirements with regard to acceptable font style and size, spacing, margins, and style (APA or MLA).

Checklist for Your Paper

Reviewing this checklist might improve your paper and your grade. Does your paper:

get your readers' attention in the opening paragraph?

state your thesis and preview your main points in your opening paragraph?

present ideas in an organized and logical manner?

sound coherent? Do ideas make sense and hang together?

have a topic sentence in each paragraph and other complete sentences that logically follow to make a point?

develop ideas with adequate support for the points made?

use transitions to help the reader understand the movement from one idea to another?

have an interesting and summative conclusion that reviews the main points and brings closure?

use the required sources (kind and number)?

cite all sources in the proper style?

mark direct quotations appropriately?

credit paraphrases and ideas of others?

have no spelling and grammar errors?

include a cover page (if required) with title, your name, professor's name, course number and section, and date?

conform to the deadline?

adhere to requirements for length, spacing, fonts, and any additional instructions on the assignment sheet?

Timeline for a Term Paper

Postponing a writing assignment is a plan for disaster. It's not likely that you will be able to put together a decent paper if you start a day or two before the deadline. Use a calendar or day planner to plot the day the assignment is due and then work backward to design a workable timeline of activities needed to complete the paper. For a term paper, create a semester plan. Adjust your timetable accordingly for shorter writing assignments that may not require as much research. Always allow time to revise and rewrite. The Assignment Calculator (www.lib.umn.edu/help/calculator) prompts you to plug in the date your paper is due and displays a day-planner guide to work on this assignment. Each step of the way you can click on tools to help you organize your thoughts, create a plan, and locate detailed tips.

As you proceed, save your work frequently, and always make a copy of your work so you never lose all of it. Too many students have learned this lesson the hard way with a low grade to prove it.

For a research paper due the 14th week of the term, your timeline might look like this:

Weeks 2–3

✓ **Know your assignment**. Read the assignment carefully and ask questions if you are not sure what the process and the final product should look like.

✓ **Update your research skills**. Students are often unaware of the resources in their university library. What resources—journals, books, databases, special collections—do you have access to? Don't think you have to discover these on your own: get to know the reference librarian and ask for help.

✓ **Choose your topic.** If the professor is assigning topics, get yours as early as you can. If there is a list to choose from, pick yours early. If the topic is your choice, make sure your instructor agrees that it fits the assignment. See Chapter 11 of *Understanding Human Communication* for advice on choosing a topic. When you've identified a likely topic, do a quick search to see if there seems to be enough information. Narrow your topic. Make sure it can be covered properly in a paper of the length assigned for the project.

Weeks 4–5

✓ **Develop a research question** that specifically asks the question you are trying to answer through your research. Careful wording of the question helps you organize and plan your research and, later, your writing.

✓ **Clarify the kinds of research required**. Professors may allow only scholarly (peer-reviewed) journals or may require a certain number or percentage be scholarly. The number and type of websites allowed may be limited. Know before you begin so you use your time wisely.

✓ **Devise your research strategy** by working with a reference librarian to find the information you need. Ask about indexes, catalogs, databases, and Internet resources. Keep records of the sources (databases, key words, websites) you've researched so you don't duplicate your efforts.

✓ **Critically review and evaluate your sources**. See Web references in the Internet Resources section to help you with this.

✓ **Take notes and create a working outline.** Careful notes help you avoid plagiarism and clarify what is or isn't another person's work. Be consistent with a system to indicate whether you have exact quotes, paraphrases, or ideas from another person.

✓ **Record your sources in the required format** so that you can properly cite them in your references or works-cited list. Know what style is required for your final paper and cite your sources in that format now. This will save hours of backtracking later to find a part of the citation you'd forgotten. Most communication courses will use APA or MLA styles; references for both are in the Internet Resources section beginning on page 33.

✓ **Broaden or narrow your topic** depending on the amount of information you find.

Weeks 7–9

✓ **Create a thesis statement and outline.** When you have much of the information you need, develop a thesis and main points in complete sentences, and note where your research will be inserted to develop your points. Your outline helps you see what pieces of information are missing and what sections require more research.

✓ **Continue your research** to round out your paper.

Weeks 10–11

✓ **Begin writing** when you have all of your information and your outline. As you write, focus on answering your research question.

✓ **Follow the technical requirements** for the paper. Read the assignment or check with the professor to be certain about the spacing, font size, margins, style (APA or MLA), and cover required.

✓ **Revise and rewrite.** Allow time to seek help from your professor, TA, writing lab, or tutor. Be certain to print a hard copy and create a backup of everything at this point. Back up your work each time you revise.

Weeks 12–13

✓ **Proofread.** Ask others to read your paper for coherence and to spot any errors.

✓ **Finish** your paper at least two days before the due date to allow for computer crashes and printer problems. Print a copy and proofread the hard copy. This also guarantees having something in hand, should you experience a technology failure.

CLASSROOM CIVILITY

You'll be more successful in this and other classes if you accept the responsibilities that come with being a student.

1.   **Know the rules of the course.** Check your syllabus; it generally spells out what you can expect in the class and what's expected of you. Since no two classes have identical rules, you can save yourself grief and boost the odds of success by investing time in reading the syllabus for every class. Some professors even give a pop quiz on the contents of the syllabus.

2.   **Attend each class.** Attendance plays an important part in college success, and students who don't skip class have several advantages: they hear explanations of assignments and changes in assignments, due dates, or test dates. They hear test reviews, they can ask questions, and they often gain an edge if a grade is borderline. Attendance attests to your seriousness as a student and your willingness to take responsibility for your learning. In a communication class such as this, participation in class activities often accounts for learning the skills and is part of the assessment (grade) for the course, as well.

3.   **Show up on time**. In some cultures and some high schools, being tardy is accepted, but the culture of college classrooms is that classes start on time and you're tardy (or marked absent) if you're not there for the start of class.

4.   **Come prepared**. Check the syllabus and be sure you read the assigned chapters before class. You'll be prepared for quizzes, activities based on the reading, and lectures. You'll also understand more from the lectures.

5.   **Accept responsibility: What you do (and don't do).** If you're absent from a class, find out what you missed from your professor or other students before the next meeting and do what's necessary to stay caught up. If the syllabus clearly tells you to check the website and not to contact the professor to find out what you've missed, follow that advice. Turn in work on time. If an assignment is late, acknowledge that fact. Excuses usually won't impress your professor, who has probably heard them all before.

Another way to accept responsibility is to avoid the "you" language described in Chapter 8. For example, instead of attacking your professor by saying, "You didn't explain this very well," use "I" language and say, "I didn't understand. . . ."

6.   **Behave in a civil manner.** Since you don't want to antagonize your professor and fellow students, follow the basic rules of civil behavior in groups. Show up on time to class. Turn off your cell phone and pager. Don't hold side conversations or butt into a lecture or discussion without being recognized first.

7.   **Show your interest.** Even if you aren't constantly fascinated by what's happening in class, acting the part of an interested student will make a good impression; and often acting interested may even help you feel more engaged. Nonverbal indicators that you are interested include leaning forward, making eye contact, smiling, nodding responsively and appropriately, asking sincere and thoughtful questions, and volunteering for activities if

asked. These behaviors will likely enhance your own learning and that of your classmates. In addition, you will help to create a supportive classroom climate.

Ask questions. If you don't understand, ask. Ask in a way that does not create defensiveness or take unnecessary class time. If something has been explained, try to identify the specific point you don't understand, rather than ask for the whole topic to be repeated. Specific questions, such as asking the professor to differentiate between two points, "Could you explain when self-concept and self-esteem are different?" or asking for an example, "Could you give an example of how self-concept and self-esteem differ?" will help you more than a general request like, "Can you go over self-concept and self-esteem again?" As you study, prepare questions that delve deeper into the material, questions that will help you understand. If you feel uncomfortable or if there is no opportunity to ask in class, try to ask the professor after class, during office hours, or by e-mail. The important thing is to ask.

Avoid behaviors that say you're *not* interested in class: text-messaging, reading another book, talking, rummaging through your pack or purse, putting your head down, sleeping, and so forth. You get the picture.

8.   **Treat others with respect in class discussions.** Listen to other points of view. Part of classroom civility is hearing and responding appropriately to others' opinions. Classrooms are marketplaces of ideas; prepare to hear and listen to opinions different from yours.

Understand others before responding. Before you respond to someone else, be sure you've understood his or her point of view. Use perception checks (Chapter 3) and paraphrases (Chapter 5) to clarify what the other has said before you respond. Use these skills to ensure that you don't embarrass yourself with a lengthy disagreement, only to find that you had misunderstood the point.

In your own comments, avoid acting dogmatic when you are actually expressing your opinion. Rather than saying, "Women are . . ." or "Men are . . .," use the phrase, "In my opinion, women are . . ." or "In my experience, men are. . . ." This shows that you understand the difference between facts, opinions, and inferences—concepts covered in Chapter 4. Other phrases that can help you be clear about recognizing that what you are saying is your own opinion, not absolute fact, are "I have learned . . . ," "I have come to believe . . . ," "I am convinced . . . ," or "I have concluded. . . ." This sort of language is less likely to trigger defensiveness than dogmatic statements. You can help reduce defensiveness and build a positive communication climate (Chapter 8).

9.   **Stay positive**. Approach the class with a positive attitude, and never take out your frustration on the professor or other students. Stating that you're frustrated is okay but unnecessary. Stating "I want to be sure I understand this" or "I want to learn this" can serve as a positive affirmation for you, your professor, and your classmates. You will generally get a more positive reaction than if you begin on a negative note like, "This is really hard. I don't know how you expect us to remember all these key terms." Focus on your goals. If your goal is to learn and to understand, stay focused on that. For more details about positive thinking benefits for students, see www.marin.cc.ca.us/~don/Study/Hcontents.html.

10.   **Recognize that success takes work.** Joining a class is like signing up for a gym membership; even though you're a "customer," you will benefit only if you follow the plan your coach (i.e., your professor) sets out for you. Commit to showing up for your classes (workouts) ready to do what it takes to tone up your understanding.

How well are you doing? Use the Classroom Savvy Checklist to find out. www.mtsu.edu/~studskl/savylist.htm.

INTERNET RESOURCES

Attention Deficit Disorder

Causes, characteristics, treatment, and legal issues plus strategies for coping, studying, and learning:

> http://www.ucc.vt.edu/academic_support_students/attention_deficit_disorder_handbook/index.html

Avoiding Plagiarism

www.indiana.edu/~wts/pamphlets/plagiarism.shtml
http://gervaseprograms.georgetown.edu/honor/system/53377.html

Classroom Savvy Checklist

www.mtsu.edu/~studskl/savylist.htm

Cornell Note Taking

www.bucks.edu/~specpop/Cornl-ex.htm

Evaluating Sources

https://owl.english.purdue.edu/owl/resource/553/01/

Learning Styles

www.vark-learn.com

Marking Texts

http://www.utexas.edu/student/utlc/lrnres/handouts/1420.html

Mind and Concept Mapping

How to mind map with sample: www.mindtools.com/mindmaps.html
How to mind map: www.peterussell.com/MindMaps/HowTo.html
Outline/example of mind mapping: www.bucks.edu/~specpop/sem-map.htm
Examples of web, tree, chart, chain, sketch:

> www.bucks.edu/~specpop/vis-org-ex.htm#web

Concept mapping:
> http://www.utc.edu/walker-center-teaching-learning/faculty-development/online-resources/cm-cd.php

Concept mapping homepage: http://users.edte.utwente.nl/lanzing/cm_home.htm

Overcoming Procrastination Self-Help Program

http://www.utexas.edu/student/utlc/class/mkg_grd/pselfhelp.html

SQ3R

www.studygs.net/texred2.htm
www.arc.sbc.edu/sq3r.html
www.teach-nology.com/web_tools/graphic_org/sq3r/

Test-Taking Skills

http://www.studygs.net/essayterms.htm

Writing Assistance

http://owl.english.purdue.edu/handouts/index.html

Writing Papers

www.lib.umn.edu/help/calculator

Writing Styles

APA: http://writing.wisc.edu/Handbook/DocAPA.html
MLA: http://www.ccc.commnet.edu/library/mla/format.shtml

Chapter 1
Communication: What and Why?

Chapter 1: Mind Map Template

To read the guide to using this mind map and see an example, refer to page 18 of the manual.

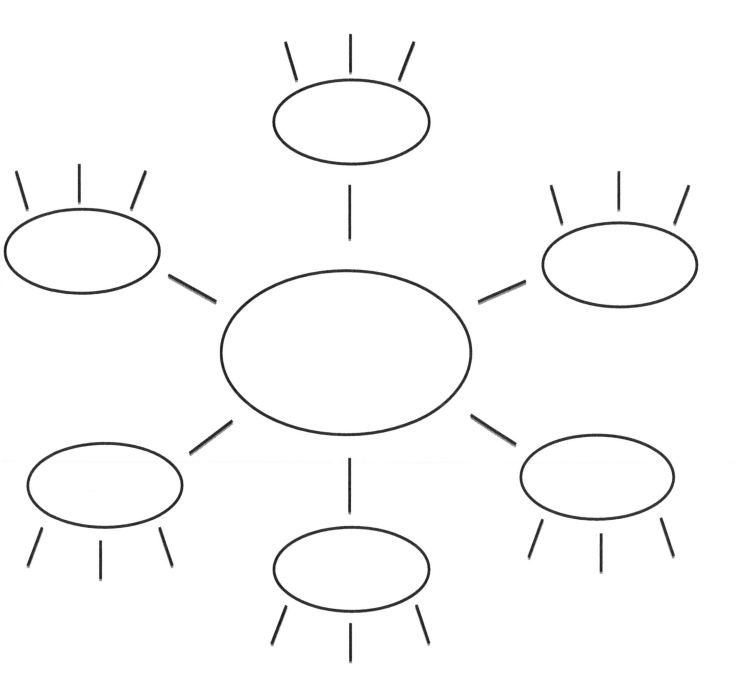

Chapter 1: Outline

Fill in the blank with a key glossary term from the word bank provided. For a completed outline, please refer to Appendix A: Chapter Outlines, beginning on page 165

    I.   _____ defined: the process of creating meaning through _____ interaction.

        A. A _____of people interacting uses _____ (including _____ _____) to convey _____ from different fields of experiences (_____). This is similar to exchanging injections of communication back and forth.

        B. A _____ _____ shows both sending and _____ is simultaneous. At any given moment we are capable of receiving, _____, and responding and overcoming _____ at the same time the other communicator is receiving, decoding, and responding while overcoming noise.

    II. Characteristics of communication: It is a symbolic relational process, not individual (not something we do to others but rather something we do with others). We use things, processes, ideas, and events arbitrarily with agreed-upon linguistic rules and customs to make communication possible.

    III. Types of communication include _____, _____, _____ _____, organizational, _____, and _____.

    IV. Communication challenges abound in this changing world. Technology has replaced face-to-face speech as the primary form of communication for today's college student.

        A. _____ _____ differs from mass communication in the variable size of the target audience. While mediated communication and face-to-face share many similarities there are differences in _____, _____ _____, and permanence. Social media is used for information, relationships, personal identity, and entertainment.

        B. To communicate competently with social media you must choose the best medium, be careful what you post, be considerate, balance with face time, and be safe.

    V. Communication is used to satisfy physical, identity, social, and practical needs.

    VI. Effective communicators have _____ _____.

        A. Communication competence is defined as achieving one's goals in a manner that, ideally, maintains or enhances the relationship in which it occurs.

        B. There is no one "ideal" way to communicate because competence is situational and relational at the same time.

        C. Competence can be learned providing the student is open to a wide range of behaviors, has the ability to choose the most appropriate behavior, develops skill at performing these behaviors, and employs empathy and perspective taking with the cognitive complexity to construct a variety of frameworks for viewing an issue. Self-monitoring and commitment to the relationship are also necessary for effective communication competence.

VII. Recognizing what communication is "not" helps avoid misconceptions.
    A. Communication does not always require complete comprehension nor will it solve all problems.
    B. Communication is not simple and more is not always better.
    C. Very often the "meaning" of communication rests in people, not in words.

Word Bank:

channels	communication
communication competence	decoding
linear model	dyadic/interpersonal
environments	intrapersonal
mass	mediated communication
messages	noise
public	receiving
richness	small group
social media	symbolic
synchronous communication	transactional model

Key Glossary Terms

For each of these terms, define the term, give an example, and explain the significance of the term.

asynchronous communication	channel
communication competence	communication
decoding	disinhibition
dyad	dyadic communication
encoding	environment
feedback	flaming
interpersonal communication	intrapersonal communication
linear communication model	mass communication
mediated communication	message
noise	public communication
receiver	richness
sender	small group communication
social media	symbol
synchronous communication	transactional communication model
Web 2.0	

Chapter 1: Review Questions

These questions are designed to help you understand this chapter's concepts and express your understanding in your own words. For practice with more questions use the course website at www.oup.com/us/adler. For answers to these questions, please refer to *Appendix B: Review Questions*, beginning on page 194.

1. After reviewing the chapter content, how would you revise your Self-Assessment answers on the Communication Choices chart featured in this chapter?

2. Define communication and identify its key characteristics.

3. What are the similarities shared by mediated and face-to-face communication? What are the major differences?

4. List one example of each of the types of communication identified in this chapter.

5. Cite the needs satisfied by communication and give an example of each.

6. Define communication competence and identify the characteristics of a competent communicator.

7. Sometime within the past day you have had a dyadic communication. Diagram the process using a transactional model.

8. Identify three dyadic communications where, as a result of the relationship involved, you have used self-monitoring to adapt and adjust your message in the midst of the exchange.

Chapter 1: Thinking Outside the Box: Synthesizing Your Knowledge

These questions are designed to stimulate critical thinking applications by blending what you've learned in this chapter with everyday applications. For answers to these questions, please refer to Appendix C: Thinking Outside the Box Questions, beginning on page 215.

1. Briefly journal a "media fast." How long can you go without mediated communication? Avoid all print, electronic, Internet, and social media. Record your experiences, feelings, the negative effects and the positive effects of using only face-to-face interaction. Ask someone **at least** twenty years your senior to attempt the same "media fast" but in reverse (i.e., he or she must use only mediated communication and no face-to-face). After a twenty-four-hour period, compare experiences.

2. Keep a journal of the frequency of your mediated communication over eight hours of your typical day. How many times in those eight hours did you use mediated communication? In those instances, why did you not use face-to-face communication instead? On a scale of 1 to 10 (with 10 = urgent and 1 = no reason, just making noise), rank your last ten mediated communication exchanges according to importance.

3. Go to www.oup.com/us/adler and select any movie listed in the Chapter 1 material. Go to the "For Further Exploration" section of Chapter 1 in the student resources section of the companion website and ask yourself: Why do you think the film listed is recommended as an example illustrating the concepts from this chapter? Explain your answer.

4. Consider someone with whom you have had a disagreement. It can be regarding politics, religion, social issues, money, or sports. Which of the following communication approaches would you feel most comfortable using:

   a. Set a designated time to talk to the person face-to-face.
   b. Call the person and settle the matter over the phone.
   c. Send an e-mail and wait for a response.
   d. Text the individual.

Explain the reasons for the avenue you chose.

Online Activities

1. Pick a debatable/controversial topic that matters to you. Some examples include religion, politics, sports, fashion, music, movies, bullying, school dress codes, a tax on oversized soft drinks, or the popularity of celebrities on reality shows. Pick a side of the debate. Prepare to discuss it on an Internet discussion board or social media platform. It can be Gmail/Gchat, Twitter, a blog, or some other outlet. Find at least two credible sources that support your point of view and during your online discussion insert the sources into your discussion. Take note of the number of people who disagreed with you who, like you, noted credible sources. Also take note of the number of people who disagreed with you who used only their personal opinions over the course of the discussion. What was the tone of the communication in each of those interactions? Do you think they would have used the same words and/or approach in a face-to-face discussion? Explain your answer.

2. Go to YouTube and watch the full version of Abbott and Costello in "Who's On First." Apply the Chapter 1 "Characteristics of Competent Communicators" to the person explaining the names of the ball players. For example:
    a. Did he pick from a wide range of behaviors to improve his chances of communication success?
    b. Did he possess the ability to choose the most appropriate behavior? Why did you understand the names but not other individuals involved in the communication?

Do the same for the other "Characteristics of Competent Communicators."

Name: _____
Date: _____

Chapter 1: Worksheet #1

1. Define communication.

2. Define communication competence.

3. What "needs" are addressed with communication?

4. Four broad categories of the use of media are identified in Chapter 1. What are those four categories?

5. Describe three guidelines for being an effective communicator via social media.

6. Many people have misconceptions about what constitutes communication. What are four things communication is "not"?

(To download this worksheet as a Word document, visit the companion website at www.oup.com/us/adler.)

Name: _____
Date: _____

Chapter 1: Worksheet #2

1. Identify the different types of communication and give a personal example of each.

2. Explain the difference between the functions of social media and mass communication. Give at least three examples.

3. Communication competence is complicated. Identify six characteristics that are common denominators in effective communication.

4. The text states that the "meaning" of messages often "rests in people, not words." Cite four examples.

(To download this worksheet as a Word document, visit the companion website at www.oup.com/us/adler.)

Chapter 2
The Self, Perception, and Communication

Chapter 2: Mind Map Template

To read the guide to using this mind map and see an example, refer to page 18 of the manual.

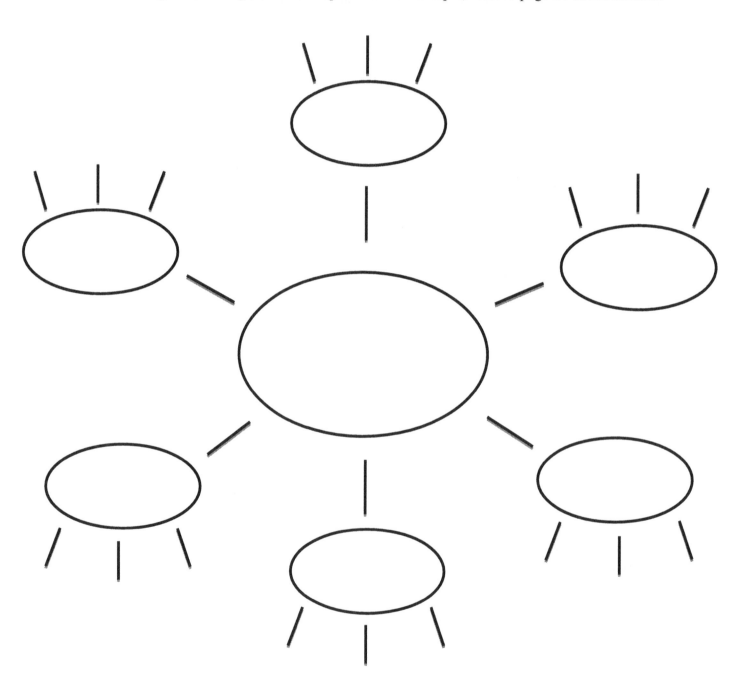

Chapter 2: Outline

Fill in the blank with a key glossary term from the word bank provided. For a completed outline, please refer to Appendix A: Chapter Outlines, beginning on page 165.

I. Nothing is more fundamental to understanding how we communicate than our sense of self.
    A. _____is the relatively stable perceptions that each of us holds about ourselves. This mental mirror reflects our view of our "self."
    B. Personality is the characteristic ways you think and behave across a variety of situations. The _____ _____ describes how you develop an image of your "self" from the way you think others view you. We particularly value the opinion of our _____ _____ as vital to our _____.

II. Our self-concept affects our behavior, which in turn affects how others view us, and we read that reaction and apply it to our self-concept.
    A. The _____ _____occurs when a person expects an outcome and behaves in a way to make the outcome more likely to occur.
    B. The self-fulfilling prophecy is an important force in communication as we often behave how we perceive others expect us to behave, thus reinforcing the perception.

III. Just like others' perception of us often influences our interaction, our perception of others affects our interaction with them.
    A. We use a _____ process to collect data for our perception. We pay attention to contrasts and change, we have motives, and we are influenced by moods.
    B. We arrange the information we gather in an _____, classifying people according to physical constructs, role constructs, interaction constructs, and psychological constructs.
    C. Our_____offers some sense of our perceptions. The degree of involvement, relational satisfaction, personal experience, assumptions, expectations, and knowledge all influence interpretation.
    D. The negotiation of this collected data is influenced by physiological things such as age, health and nutrition, biological factors, and neurology.
    E. Cultural influences provide a filter for interpretation. Sex and gender roles also affect perception; so too do occupational and relational roles.
    F. We all have our own story, our_____: a framework of explaining behavior and shaping communication.

IV. Shared narratives may be desirable but are hard to achieve. Often we undertake the process of attaching meaning to behavior. This attribution leads to some common perceptual tendencies.

    A. We make snap judgments based on_____. We judge ourselves more charitably than we judge others, we pay more attention to negative impressions than positive ones, and we are influenced by what is most obvious.

    B. We also err when we cling to first impressions even if later proved wrong, and we tend to assume others similar to us are "like" us.

V. One solution to overcoming these tendencies is to have the ability to apply _____.

    A. Perspective taking gives us the ability to take on the other's viewpoint. While not to be confused with _____, empathy identifies with the other. Empathy allows for understanding without requiring you to agree with the reasons.

    B. Good intentions and empathy are best used to handle _____ _____. This involves describing the behavior, offering at least two interpretations, and making a request for clarification.

VI. The communication strategies people use to influence how others view them are called _____ _____.

    A. Our _____ _____ is a reflection of self-concept—who, in moments of honest reflection, we believe we are. Our _____ _____ is the way we want to appear to others.

    B. The term _____ is used to describe the presenting self and _____is the verbal and nonverbal ways we maintain our presenting image.

    C. We have multiple identities we present in a multiple of settings. We perform in tandem with others, we collaborate, as we sometimes think we are expected to perform.

    D. We do this both consciously and unconsciously; sometimes we are aware of the image we are projecting but at other times we slip into roles without planning or consciously trying. We differ in the degree of identity management depending on our self-monitoring.

VII. We usually manage our identities to follow social rules.

    A. Social rules govern our behaviors as we strive to meet expectations and to accomplish personal goals.

    B. While mediated communication limits the potential for accurate perception it is used for identity management. Strangers change their age, history, personality, and even gender. This form of deception, known as "cat-fishing," gained national prominence recently with the exposé of a fraud perpetuated on a nationally known collegiate football figure.

    C. There is a fine line between managing identities and remaining honest. The decision must come from within as complete self-disclosure, absolute blunt honesty, is rarely appropriate.

Word Bank

empathy	face
facework	identify management
interpretation	narrative
organization	perceived self
presenting self	reflected appraisal
selection	Self-concept
self-esteem	self-fulfilling prophecy
significant others	stereotyping
sympathy	

Key Glossary Terms

For each of these terms, define the term, give an example, and explain the significance of the term.

attribution	empathy
ethnocentrism	face
facework	identity management
interpretation	narrative
organization	perceived self
perception checking	presenting self
reflected appraisal	selection
self-concept	self-esteem
self-fulfilling prophecy	self-serving bias
significant other	stereotyping
sympathy	

Chapter 2: Review Questions

These questions are designed to help you understand this chapter's concepts and express your understanding in your own words. For practice with more questions use the course website at www.oup.com/us/adler. For answers to these questions, please refer to *Appendix B: Review Questions*, beginning on page 194.

1. What are the communicative influences that shape the self-concept?

2. Define self-concept and list, in one minute's time, as many characteristics as possible describing you.

3. What is the connection between the phenomenon of the self-fulfilling prophecy and your personal success or failure in performing a challenging task?

4. The text identifies several common perceptual tendencies that, through attribution, often cause inaccurate and troublesome perceptions. List these errors.

5. Empathy has three dimensions. Explain your process of perspective-checking, emotional dimension, and genuine concern when a student enters the classroom and awkwardly slips and falls.

6. Define identity management. Put yourself in a job interview situation and identify the choices made in the characteristics of identity management.
    a. Of your multiple identities, which one do you exhibit?
    b. Who is involved in the collaborative process?
    c. What conscious indicators are present?
    d. What unconscious tendencies are communicated between you and the interviewer?
    e. Once you have selected a certain identity, how do you self-monitor?

Is this process ethical? Explain your answer.

7. What tools are the most common influences on perception in mediated communication?

8. Is honesty always the best policy? Explain your answer.

Chapter 2: Thinking Outside the Box: Synthesizing Your Knowledge.

These questions are designed to stimulate critical thinking applications by blending what you've learned in this chapter with everyday applications. For answers to these questions, please refer to Appendix C: Thinking Outside the Box Questions, beginning on page 215.

1. A job application asks you to list your faults and your strengths. How do you match your self-concept to the presenting self that others view in such a way to be honest but not ruin your chances?

2. Watch the movie "Precious." Watch the movie "Temple Grandin." Watch the movie "Fast and Furious." Describe the effect perceptual errors have on the communication decisions others made toward Precious and Temple. Pay particular attention to the character Dominic in "Fast and Furious." What identity was reflected by others to Dominic?

3. Have you ever been deceitful or misleading regarding the "you" presented via social media? Do you find yourself braver, more outspoken, more expressive in online communication channels? Which medium—face-to-face or mediated communication— causes you greater discomfort when being honest? Why?

4. At family gatherings, is it typical to share stories? Are past family episodes, incidents, and anecdotes told and retold? Are newcomers to the family and/or visiting guests expected to appreciate and process these narratives to better understand your family and your culture? Write down a few of these narratives and identify their common themes and patterns. What might guests or newcomers take away from these narratives?

Online Activities

1.Investigate three websites dealing with bullying and, citing where you got your information, summarize the root causes of bullying.

2. Interviewing for jobs can be awkward and uncomfortable because your perceived self and presenting self are often at conflict throughout the process. How do you manage this tension? Use Internet sources and make two lists for job interviewees: "ten things to do" and "ten things not to do" when applying and interviewing for jobs. Compare your lists with two classmates, then collaborate to compile a final list to present to the class.

Name: _____

Date: _____

Chapter 2: Worksheet #1

1. Define self-concept.

2. Identify five common erroneous perceptual tendencies.

3. Define empathy.

4. What are the characteristics of identity management?

5. List and analyze three situations where absolute honesty might not be the best policy.

(To download this worksheet as a Word document, visit the companion website at www.oup.com/us/adler.)

Name: _____
Date: _____

Chapter 2: Worksheet #2

1. What are the two types of self-fulfilling prophecies? Provide an example of each.

2. What factors influence perception?

3. What are the three dimensions of empathy?

4. Name ethical justifications for managing identities.

5. Make a list of six or seven traits that best describe your perceived self.

(To download this worksheet as a Word document, visit the companion website at www.oup.com/us/adler.)

Chapter 3
Communication and Culture

Chapter 3: Mind Map Template

To read the guide to using this mind map and see an example, refer to page 18 of the manual.

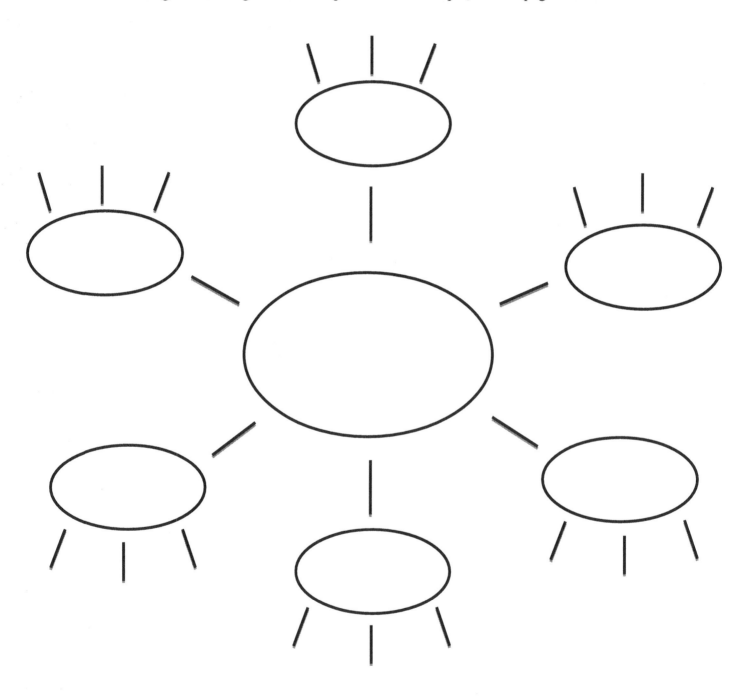

Chapter 3: Outline

Fill in the blank with a key glossary term from the word bank provided. For a completed outline, please refer to Appendix A: Chapter Outlines, beginning on page 165.

I. Defining _____ is not easy. The simplest definition is to say it is the language, values, beliefs, traditions, and customs people share and learn.
    A. _____ is a group within the culture. Membership in a coculture often shapes the nature of communication.
    B. _____ describes the weight we attach to cultural characteristics.
II. Cultural differences are generalizations but cultural values and norms shape communication.
    A. Cultures valuing the individual more are said to be _____, whereas _____ _____ put group above self. Two distinct ways members of various cultures deliver messages are _____ _____ and ___ _____.
    B. Cultures have ways of coping with unpredictable situations. The level of _____ _____ reflects reaction to ambiguous circumstances.
The extent of the gap between social groups who possess resources and those who don't is called _____ _____ . Greater or lesser power distance signals class separation or class equality.
    C. Some cultures value silence in communication whereas others insert talking as required social acceptance. There is a tendency to regard some cultures as masculine, feminine, and androgynous.
    D. Race and ethnicity mostly involve superficial qualities but have social significance. _____ and _____ often accompany noted differences between ethnicities and race. Regional differences shape feelings of belonging and are often indicated via accents.
    E. Cultures attach communicative value in gender identity and sexual orientation, religion, physical ability or disability, age, and socioeconomic status.
III. Different verbal and nonverbal communication codes hamper cross-cultural communication.
    A. Language and identity are closely tied to prestige.
    B. Verbal codes such as directness or indirectness, elaborate or succinct, and formality or informality affect characterizations and perceptions.
    C. Nonverbal codes offer a range of interpretations and symbolism. Proximity, eye contact, touch, volume, and gestures are all measured with an eye toward culture.
IV. Decoding the verbal and nonverbal systems across cultures is a challenge.
    A. Translation does not guarantee clarity.
    B. Comprehending patterns of thought is more important than literal translation.

V. The best development of intercultural communication competence hinges on a wide range of appropriate behaviors.
   A. Increased contact produces contact hypothesis and better relationships.
   B. A tolerance for ambiguity averts fear and apprehension of the "different."
   C. Open-mindedness can combat _____ : the attitude that one's culture is superior to another.
   D. Education, knowledge, and skill are developed through passive observation, active strategies, and self-disclosure.
   E. Most of all, patience and perseverance reward the effort. Culture shock or adjustment shock causes confusion, disorientation, resentment, and disappointment. Have patience. Continue the effort.

Word Bank

coculture	collectivistic culture
culture	ethnocentrism
high context	individualistic
low context	power distance
prejudice	salience
stereotyping	uncertainty avoidance

Key Glossary Terms

For each of these terms, define the term, give an example, and explain the significance of the term.

coculture	collectivistic culture
culture	ethnocentrism
high-context culture	in-groups
individualistic culture	intergroup communication
low-context culture	out-groups
power distance	prejudice
salience	stereotyping
uncertainty avoidance	

Chapter 3: Review Questions

These questions are designed to help you understand this chapter's concepts and express your understanding in your own words. For practice with more questions use the course website at www.oup.com/us/adler. For answers to these questions, please refer to *Appendix B: Review Questions*, beginning on page 194.

1. Identify how cultures and cocultures play a significant role in your social sphere, and in society at large.

2. Give examples illustrating when cultural and cocultural factors play a role in communication.

3. Can you distinguish between overgeneralizations and actual cultural/cocultural differences in communication?

4. Explain and give examples of cultural values, norms, and cultural/cocultural codes that shape and affect communication.

5. Identify verbal and nonverbal codes that govern communication in a culture of your choosing.

6. Use the self-assessment criteria in this chapter to gauge your intercultural communication competence. In what ways could you improve?

7. Identify the unique ingredients of intercultural communication competence.

8. Compare and contrast the responses you would likely receive if you said the following in low-context versus high-context cultures:
   a) I wish you would not scratch there in public.
   b) The food you prepared and served me tastes horrible.
   c) Please say you want to go out with me, please.

Chapter 3: Thinking Outside the Box: Synthesizing Your Knowledge.

These questions are designed to stimulate critical thinking applications by blending what you've learned in this chapter with everyday applications. For answers to these questions, please refer to Appendix C: Thinking Outside the Box Questions, beginning on page 215.

1. Review clips from the television show "Modern Family." Identify the cultures, cocultures, in-groups, out-groups, and intercultural communication challenges in the fictional family depicted in the show. Now compare and contrast them with your own family.

2. Attend a meeting or gathering of individuals from a culture or coculture outside your comfort zone. Observe the use of verbal and nonverbal codes and the social interactions in play. Do you become more comfortable and understandable over time? Explain.

3. Businesses and organizations have a unique coculture that new employees must learn to navigate. Interview a supervisor and an experienced employee. List language, values, beliefs, traditions, practices, and norms unique to their coculture.

4. Interview two or three people who graduated from high school in the 1960's. Compile a list of cultural idioms spoken by baby-boomers when they were teenagers. Phrases such as "a gas", "to go ape" " a blast" , "to book", "cool cat", "to ditch something", "scarf", and "wicked". What are the definitions of these phrases and expressions per the baby-boomers? Translate the terminology to equivalent phrases used by teens today. Which adage best describes the results: "The more things change the more they stay the same" or "You just don't understand"? Explain your answer.

Online Activities

1. Find a website, blog, Facebook page, or discussion board where you can interact with individuals who live in other countries. If it helps to announce this is a school project, then do so. Prepare a short list of traits you value from your culture—it can be dating norms, achievements and accomplishments, interests and hobbies, religious practices, favorite foods, holiday activities, music preferences, use of cell phones for socialization, parental oversight, hopes and aspirations for the future. Ask other participants to do the same. Exchange lists. Are there notable cultural differences? Explain.

2. Create a timeline using the years 1850, 1900, 1950, 2000, and today. Using Internet sources, describe the societal communication "culture" at each of those five times in terms of the following categories: gender roles, ethnicity and race, sexual orientation, religion, physical disability, mental health issues, the elderly, and socioeconomic status (both rich and poor). Give specific examples of language used, documented incidents, historical facts, and notable people involved.

Name: _____
Date: _____

Chapter 3: Worksheet #1

1. Define culture.

2. Define salience.

3. What steps are necessary to develop intercultural communication competence?

4. Define uncertainty avoidance and provide an example.

5. Miss Nomer wants to be the number-one salesperson in her entire company. She strives for recognition, achievement, and awards. She is blunt about what she likes and doesn't like. Mr. Completely has declined the past three pay raises he has been offered, saying that the money could be better used to improve the employee break room and repair the potholes in the parking lot. He does not say if he is happy or sad and has never been heard to complain out loud. What cultural values and communication styles do these two people represent?

(To download this worksheet as a Word document, visit the companion website at www.oup.com/us/adler.)

Name: _____
Date: _____

Chapter 2: Worksheet #2

1. Identify three cultural differences in verbal style.

2. Gestures are an important part of nonverbal codes, though translation and patterns of thought affect their interpretation. What are three gestures used frequently in your coculture that could "mean" something else in another coculture?

3. Compare and contrast the "culture" of shopping at a garage sale and shopping at a high-end designer outlet.

(To download this worksheet as a Word document, visit the companion website at www.oup.com/us/adler.)

Chapter 4
Language

Chapter 4: Mind Map Template

To read the guide to using this mind map and see an example, refer to page 18 of the manual.

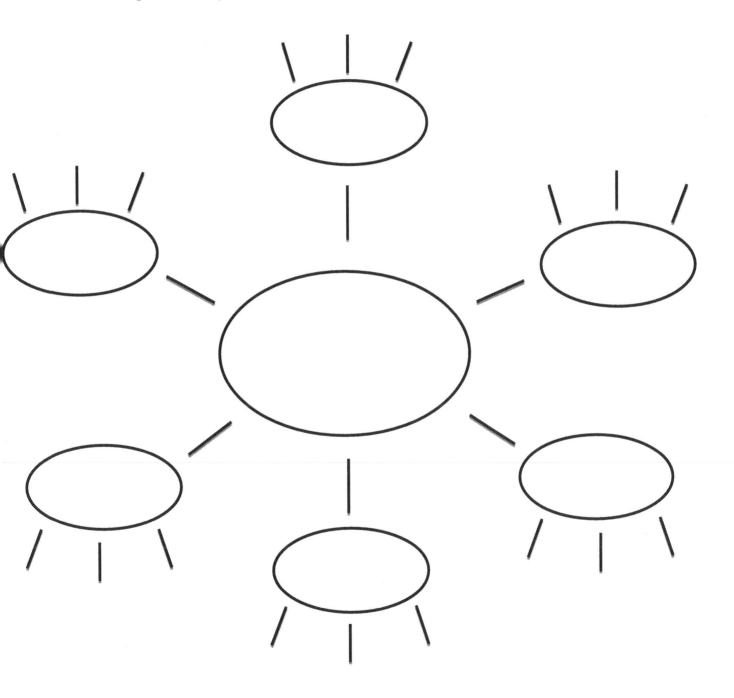

Chapter 4: Outline

Fill in the blank with a key glossary term from the word bank provided. For a completed outline, please refer to Appendix A: Chapter Outlines, beginning on page 165.

I. _____ is defined as a collection of _____ governed by rules and used to convey messages between individuals.
   A. Language is symbolic, with the meanings resting in people, not the words.
   B. Language is rule governed. _____ _____ govern sound, _____ _____ govern structure, _____ _____ deal with meaning, and _____ _____ cover interactions.
   C. The use of language shapes attitudes through naming, credibility, status, sexism, and racism.
   D. How we use language reflects back on us through power, affiliation, attraction and interest, and responsibility.
II. Most language misunderstandings are easily remedied if you recognize them.
   A. Words or phrases having more than one meaning are called _____ _____. Often misinterpreted because they can be taken "the wrong way," equivocal phrasing can also be ambiguous and misleading.
   B. _____ gain their meaning by comparison; the misunderstanding arises from variations in contrast.
   C. _____ is a language used by a group of people whose members belong to a similar coculture, whereas _____ is a specialized vocabulary that functions as a kind of shorthand for people with common knowledge or experience.
   D. Overly _____ _____ uses objects, events, and ideas to describe varying degrees of specificity. A book is not just a book: it can be hardback or paperback, a textbook or a novel, large print or on an e-reader.
   E. Abstract language refers to events or objects only vaguely. It is used to avoid confrontations, to hint, or to generalize, thus causing confusion and misunderstanding.
III. Three bad linguistic habits often result in disruptive language that stimulates trouble.
   A. Confusing facts and opinions: an _____ _____ masked as a _____ _____ leads to conflict.
   B. Confusing facts and inferences: arriving at a conclusion from interpretation and not labeling the _____ _____ as opinion leads to difficulty.
   C. Using _____ _____ that sounds descriptive but signals attitude causes problems.
IV. Evasive language is designed to mislead or antagonize. It purposefully avoids clear communication.

    A. To substitute a pleasant term for a more direct but potentially less pleasant one is to use _____.

    B. To be deliberately vague in a way that can be interpreted in more than one way is to use _____.

V. There are similarities and there are differences in how the genders use language.

    A. In terms of content, men are more likely to talk about recreation, technology, and nightlife, whereas women tend to favor discussing relationships, friends, family, and emotions.

    B. Women concentrate more on personal problems first; men joke and kid around and tease.

    C. Men use language more to accomplish a task, women to support, demonstrate, and share values.

    D. Women ask questions; men make statements.

    E. Similarities exist and the differences blur when men and women use profanity and vocal fillers, have shared occupations, and exist in mutually similar socioeconomic strata.

    F. Often psychological ___ _____ play more of a influence than biological sex in how the genders use language.

Word Bank

abstract language	emotive language
equivocal language	equivocation
euphemisms	factual statement
inferential statement	jargon
language	opinion statement
phonological rules	pragmatic rules
relative words	semantic rules
sex roles	slang
symbols	syntactic rules

Key Glossary Terms

For each of these terms, define the term, give an example, and explain the significance of the term.

abstract language	abstraction ladder
behavioral description	convergence
divergence	emotive language
equivocal language	equivocal words
equivocation	euphemism
factual statement	inferential statement
jargon	language
linguistic intergroup bias	linguistic relativism
opinion statement	phonological rules
pragmatic rules	relative words
semantic rules	sex role
slang	symbols
syntactic rules	

Chapter 4: Review Questions

These questions are designed to help you understand this chapter's concepts and express your understanding in your own words. For practice with more questions use the course website at www.oup.com/us/adler. For answers to these questions, please refer to *Appendix B: Review Questions*, beginning on page 194.

1. Define language and cite an example for each of the four rules that govern language.

2. Language shapes attitudes through at least four methods of use. Cite a "for instance" example to accompany the four methods.

3. Competent communicators realize that their use of language reflects on them and their attitudes. Identify four contributing factors that "reflect" on the sender.

4. Identify specific examples of language that often cause misunderstandings and—citing personal experience, current or historical events, etc.—explain why each is problematic.

5. Create four compare/contrast examples of the way language is used to accept or reject responsibility.

6. List three ways in which, generally speaking, men and women use language differently.

7. Complete the Self-Assessment chart titled, "Your Use of Language," from this chapter. Be honest about yourself. What did you discover from your responses?

Chapter 4: Thinking Outside the Box: Synthesizing Your Knowledge

These questions are designed to stimulate critical thinking applications by blending what you've learned in this chapter with everyday applications. For answers to these questions, please refer to Appendix C: Thinking Outside the Box Questions, beginning on page 215.

1. In theory, we value people who "tell it like it is" and we consider "beating around the bush" to be a sign of deception and avoidance. In practice, however, we often react differently. Why?

2. Read the following paragraph. Underline the offensive words and phrases. Rewrite the paragraph substituting euphemisms in place of the offensive words and phrases.

Did you hear what happened to me at the choke and puke diner? This sawed-off old witch with spikey hair sticking up like cactus bristles pointed her gnarled knobby twisted knuckles at me and, in a screeching voice that sounded like rusty hinges, said I was drunk. Can you believe that? Then she started hacking and coughing like a cat with a hairball. Next thing I knew these two rent-a-cops came up to me—one looked like he had been around since Moses came down off the mountain and the other was a snot-nosed new hire—and they barked at me to haul my bony hind-end out of there. I didn't want to eat in that roach coach anyway, so I gave them the finger and left.

3. The best way to avoid overly abstract language is to use behavioral descriptions instead. Behavioral descriptions move down the abstraction ladder to identify the specific, observable phenomenon being discussed. What three questions should a thorough description answer?

Online Activities

1. Go to YouTube and search for a video of George Carlin's "football or baseball" clip. Note his unique and creative use of language. Does the listener get a sense of Carlin's attitude toward football? Toward baseball? Explain your answer.

2. An interesting approach to highlighting language can be found on YouTube's "Phonetic Punctuation" by Victor Borge. What "rules" of language is he mocking? Explain.

3. Research the following articles on the Internet: "The Gender Similarities Hypothesis" by Janet Hyde; "The Different Using of Language Between the Sexes" by Zheng Baohua; and "Male and female language: growing together?" by Irene van Baalen. Using those articles as a foundation, write a one-page paper discussing your opinion on how to approach and understand gender differences in the use of language.

Name: _____

Date: _____

Chapter 4: Worksheet #1

1. Define language.

2. What four rules govern the use of language?

3. Identify five ways the use of language shapes attitudes.

4. Identify four ways in which your use of language reflects back on you.

5. Identify two types of evasive language that often cause confusion and misunderstandings.

6. What is the difference between slang and jargon? Give an example of each.

(To download this worksheet as a Word document, visit the companion website at www.oup.com/us/adler.)

Name: _____

Date: _____

Chapter 4: Worksheet #2

1. How strongly do you feel about certain things? The use of emphasis in language reflects back on you. See if you recognize the "attitude" reflected as you answer the following questions out loud.

    a. Name a food you absolutely love to eat. _____

    b. Identify a food you don't care for—you will eat it if you have to, move it around on your plate with your fork, but you do not care for it. _____

    c. Name a food you hate. _____

Did you notice the variation in the "power" of your answers? Describe the differences.

2. Recall a disagreement you recently had with a parent, supervisor, or co-worker that contained "loaded" statements. Give two examples of such statements and explain the inferences you or your parent, supervisor, or co-worker drew as a result.

3. We often encounter situations requiring a decision between honest and evasive language. Give an example of a situation you have encountered in which you have made such a decision. Explain your reasoning.

(To download this worksheet as a Word document, visit the companion website at www.oup.com/us/adler.)

Chapter 5
Listening

Chapter 5: Mind Map Template

To read the guide to using this mind map and see an example, refer to page 18 of the manual.

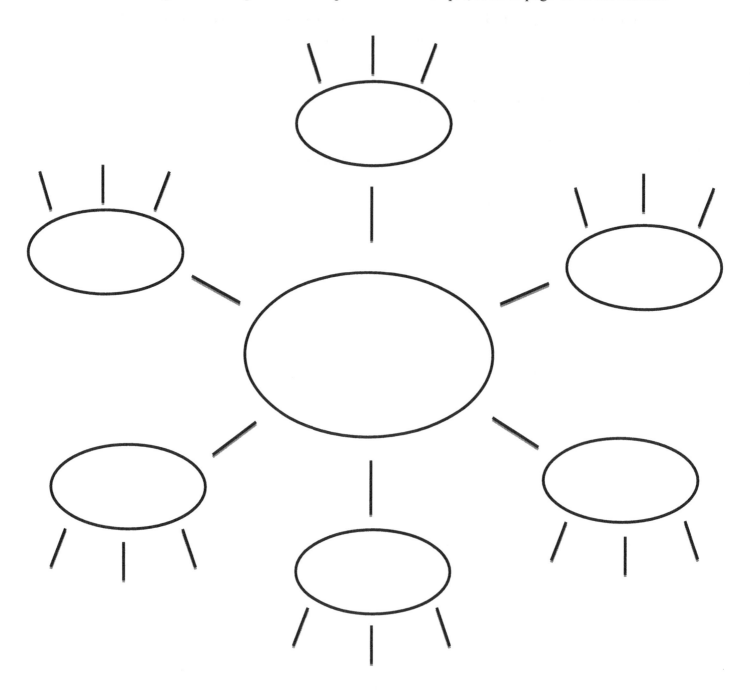

Chapter 5: Outline

Fill in the blank with a key glossary term from the word bank provided. For a completed outline, please refer to Appendix A: Chapter Outlines, beginning on page 165.

I. _____ and _____ are not the same thing.
- A. Listening occurs when the brain reconstructs electrochemical impulses into a representation of the original sound and gives them meaning.
- B. Listening requires _____, _____, _____, and _____.
- C. _____ _____ is the degree of congruence between what a listener understands and what the sender was attempting to communicate.
- D. Listening is not a natural process where all listeners receive the same message.
- E. _____ _____ requires effort whereas _____ _____ is passive with low-level processing of information.

II. There are several faulty listening behaviors we all possess.
- A. _____ is to imitate the real thing; _____ _____ responds only to a part of the message.
- B. _____ _____ turns innocent remarks into attacks and _____collects information in order to attack back.
- C. _____ listeners avoid and_____ listeners are unable to look beyond the words and take things at face value.
- D. _____ _____ takes place when listeners turn all conversations onto themselves.

III. The causes of poor listening are many.
- A. Message overload, rapid thought, and psychological and physical noise are some reasons for poor listening.
- B. Other reasons are hearing problems, faulty assumptions, talking has more advantages, cultural differences, and media influences.

IV. There are a number of reasons people invest effort into listening.
- A. _____-_____ _____ aims to be _____ _____ by looking for key ideas, asking questions, _____, and taking notes.
- B. _____ _____ aims at emotional connections by taking the time to listen for unexpressed thoughts and feelings and encouraging further comments.
- C. _____ _____ aims to enhance the relationship and understand the message. This is done by listening before evaluating, separating the message from the speaker, and searching for value.
- D. Applying analytical listening to see if a message stands up to scrutiny is one element of _____ _____. The goal here is to examine the

speaker's evidence and reasoning, gauge the speaker's credibility, and examine the emotional appeals being employed.

V. _____ _____ is aimed to help the speaker deal with personal dilemmas.

    A. Using mediated communication for counseling and advice has grown into an industry of its own for medical conditions, eating disorders, sexual orientation, divorce, shyness, addiction, loneliness, safety, and exercise because of, along with other factors, the online anonymity support avenues that prompt faster revelations in a shorter period of time.

    B. Generally speaking, women are more likely than men to give supportive responses when presented with another person's problems.

    C. Supportive responses come in the form of _____, judging, _____, _____ , _____, _____ , and reflecting.

    D. Before committing, be sure your support is welcomed. You should evaluate the situation, the other person, and your own strengths and weaknesses.

Word Bank

advising	ambushing
analytical listening	analyzing
attending	comforting
critical listening	defensive listening
hearing	informational listening
insensitive	insulated
listening	listening fidelity
mindful listening	mindless listening
paraphrasing	prompting
pseudolistening	questioning
relational listening	remembering
responding	selective listening
stage hogging	supportive listening
task-oriented listening	understanding

Key Glossary Terms

For each of these terms, define the term, give an example, and explain the significance of the term.

advising response

analytical listening

attending

content-oriented listening

critical listening

hearing

insensitive listening

judging response

listening fidelity

mindless listening

prompting

questioning

relational listening

residual message

selective listening

stage hogging

task-oriented listening

ambushing

analyzing statement

comforting

counterfeit question

defensive listening

informational listening

insulated listening

listening

mindful listening

paraphrasing

pseudolistening

reflecting

remembering

responding

sincere question

supportive listening

understanding

Chapter 5: Review Questions

These questions are designed to help you understand this chapter's concepts and express your understanding in your own words. For practice with more questions use the course website at www.oup.com/us/adler. For answers to these questions, please refer to *Appendix B: Review Questions*, beginning on page 194.

1. What are the four fundamental differences between listening and hearing? Explain your definition of mindful listening in comparison to mindless listening.

2. Identify the faulty listening behaviors described in the text and cite an example of each.

3. In addition to faulty listening behaviors there are other reasons for poor listening. The recipe for inattention and mindless listening includes both things that can be avoided with effort and some inescapable facts of life. Identify nine reasons for poor listening.

4. Take the Self-Assessment evaluation of your listening styles. What are the types of listening that you value most? Why?

5. Define task-oriented listening and identify the guidelines one must follow to be more effective with this listening technique.

6. Define relational listening and identify the necessary components of this approach. What are some of the drawbacks to this type of listening?

7. Identify the necessary components of analytical listening.

8. Being skeptical and cynical is useful with critical listening. Define this skill, and cite the procedures used by successful critical listeners.

9. Identify seven ways to respond supportively to another person's remarks.

Chapter 5: Thinking Outside the Box: Synthesizing Your Knowledge

These questions are designed to stimulate critical thinking applications by blending what you've learned in this chapter with everyday applications. For answers to these questions, please refer to Appendix C: Thinking Outside the Box Questions, beginning on page 215.

1. How well do you listen? In a small group setting of approximately 20 to 25 people, perform the following experiment:

   a. Ask everyone to pay attention and listen. A volunteer will carefully recite 15 words.

   b. The words are: Begin, Walk, Run, Study, Horsefeathers, Repeat, Corn, Easy, Listen, Maneuver, Coat, Mastication, Thirteen, Slow, Stop.

   c. After the words have been read, ask each person to write down the words in order. The goal is to see how effectively each person listened.

   d. Discuss why as a group.

2. Telephone. In a group of approximately 8 to 10 people, stand up and form a circle or a straight line. Ask one person to whisper any phrase or sentence of his or her choosing to the person next to him or her. Each person is to whisper the phrase he or she has heard to the next person in line. See if the message at the end matches the original. Discuss reasons why it did or did not.

3. Keep a journal for four hours and record the incidents of poor listening you observe around you.

Online Activities

1. Go to YouTube and view "Mr. Singh case study: Poor listening skills." What were the obstacles that caused poor listening? Now view "Magnificent Scene from the King's Speech" on the quintessentialcinema YouTube channel. What is the argument about? Why isn't Lionel Logue (played by Geoffrey Rush) allowed to sit in the chair? What factors or behaviors interfered with the king's ability to listen effectively?

2. Select a president or presidential candidate for whom you did not or would not vote. Search for and listen to one of his or her speeches on the Internet. List each faulty listening behavior you commit. Why did you listen to the speech in this way? Replay the speech and listen critically. Has your opinion of the candidate and/or the content of the speech changed? If so, how so? If not, why not?

Name: _____

Date: _____

Chapter 5: Worksheet #1

1. What are the four differences between listening and hearing?

2. Identify seven faulty listening behaviors.

3. Describe three approaches to effective paraphrasing.

4. Give three points of good advice for performing supportive listening and advising a friend in crisis.

5. Identify four forms of counterfeit questions.

(To download this worksheet as a Word document, visit the companion website at www.oup.com/us/adler.)

Name: _____
Date: _____

Chapter 5: Worksheet #2

1. What is the difference between analytical listening and critical listening?

2. What is the difference between rapid thought and psychological noise?

3. Listeners can be most helpful when they do which three things mentioned in the text?

4. Task-oriented listening is most beneficial in a classroom setting. Identify four guidelines that you should follow to become a better task-oriented listener.

(To download this worksheet as a Word document, visit the companion website at www.oup.com/us/adler.)

Chapter 6
Nonverbal Communication

Chapter 6: Mind Map Template

To read the guide to using this mind map and see an example, refer to page 18 of the manual.

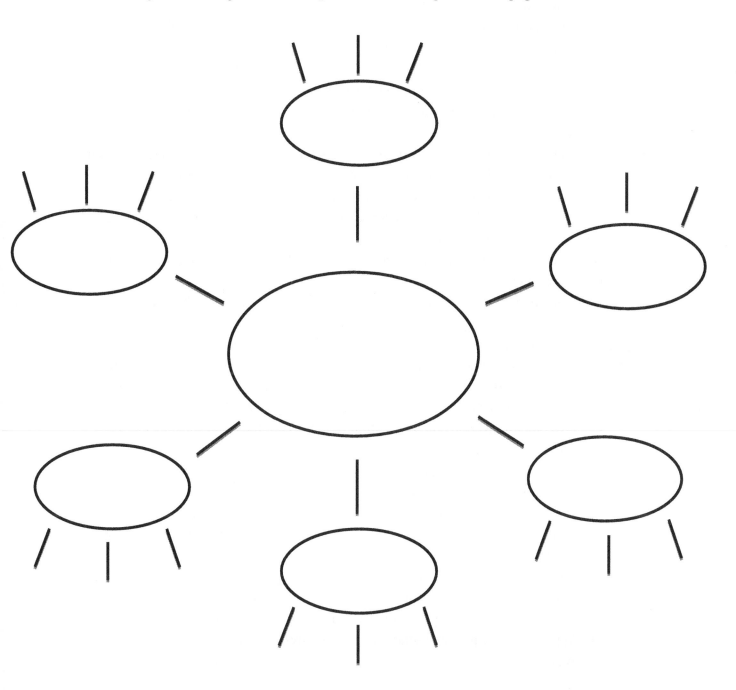

Chapter 6: Outline

Fill in the blank with a key glossary term from the word bank provided. For a completed outline, please refer to Appendix A: Chapter Outlines, beginning on page 165.

I. Messages expressed through nonlinguistic means are _____ _____.
   A. Such messages do have communicative value, although they are primarily relational.
   B. While nonverbal communication is ambiguous, it differs from verbal communication because of complexity and flow.
   C. Nonverbal encoding and decoding skills are strong predictors of popularity, attractiveness, and socioemotional well-being.
II. There are important differences in the way people use and understand nonverbal behavior.
   A. Cultures have varying nonverbal languages in gestures, the use of silence, the use of space and distance, eye contact, and even frequency of interruptions.
   B. Gender roles are often stereotypical, but generally speaking women tend to smile more, use more facial expressions, touch others more, stand closer to others, and make more eye contact.
III. Nonverbal communication functions along with verbal communication for more effective communication.
   A. Nonverbal communication uses repeating to aid in memory, substituting to communicate _____ with precise meaning within a cultural group, and complementing to reinforce or go along with verbal communication.
   B. The process of placing emphasis on oral messages is the nonverbal function of accenting. Nonverbal communication is also used for regulating—signaling the beginning or the end of communication and controlling the pace.
   C. Two other nonverbal communication functions are the often-misunderstood practice of contradicting and the usually uncomfortable art of deceiving.
IV. There are many tools at our disposal for sending nonverbal messages.
   A. Body movements are the most noticeable and include posture and gestures.
   B. The face and the eyes have powerful nonverbal impact. Expressions reflecting many emotions are called _____ _____, where two or more expressions show different emotions.
   C. One great nonverbal tool is the voice. _____ is the word used to describe nonverbal but vocal messages such as volume, emphasis, tone, speed, pitch, pauses, and any _____ such as stammering and vocal fillers.
   D. Appearance is a message sender involving physical attractiveness, clothing, and hygiene.

E. Physical touch can "speak" volumes. The use of distance and the way people and animals use space is called_____ . _____ _____ is from skin contact to about 18 inches out from the body. _____ _____ starts at about 18 inches and can go out four feet. _____ _____ starts at four feet and extends to twelve feet. _____ _____ goes from twelve feet on out. Distance is something we like to decide depending on how we feel toward the other person, the context of the conversation, and our personal goals.

F. Where personal space is our invisible bubble we carry around and adjust depending on the influences, territoriality is fixed. A room, a building, a neighborhood, or even a larger area to which we assume some kind of "rights" is our _____. "My desk," "my office," "my yard," and "my city" are typical expressions of territoriality. We grant people with higher status more personal territory and greater privacy.

G. The physical environment people create reflects and shapes nonverbal interactions, and the study of how human beings use and structure time (known as_____) expresses both intentional and unintentional messages.

V. Knowledge about nonverbal messages can improve communication skills, can allow the listener to be more attuned to others, and can make communicators more aware of the messages they send.

A. It pays to tune out words and focus on meaning, usually sent nonverbally.

B. Since nonverbal communication is ambiguous, always perform perception-checking practices.

C. Pay attention to your own nonverbal practices. Record a video of "you being you" in an average conversation and then turn off the volume. What are you "saying" by what you are "doing"? That is the message others get.

Word Bank

affect blends	chronemics
disfluency	emblems
intimate distance	nonverbal communication
paralanguage	personal distance
proxemics	public distance
social distance	territory

Key Glossary Terms

For each of these terms, define the term, give an example, and explain the significance of the term.

affect blend	affect displays
chronemics	disfluency
emblems	haptics
illustrators	intimate distance
kinesics	manipulators
microexpressions	monochromic
nonverbal communication	paralanguage
personal distance	polychromic
proxemics	public distance
social distance	territory

Chapter 6: Review Questions

These questions are designed to help you understand this chapter's concepts and express your understanding in your own words. For practice with more questions use the course website at www.oup.com/us/adler. For answers to these questions, please refer to *Appendix B: Review Questions*, beginning on page 194.

1.   Define nonverbal communication. Provide an example from personal experience of each characteristic listed.

2. List three examples of typical nonverbal communication cues, unique to your culture, that you encounter in a typical day's activities. Would they need interpretation to someone not of your culture? Explain your answer.

3. Make a list of the social factors that influence gender-oriented nonverbal communication.

4. Describe the etiquette surrounding nonverbal communication in mediated communication. How are nonverbal messages most often conveyed via today's technology?

5. Compare and contrast your use of nonverbal communication at a party with friends versus a job interview.

6. Do you lean toward a monochronic mindset and culture, or is your tendency more polychronic? Use specific examples from your experiences to support your answer.

Chapter 6: Thinking Outside the Box: Synthesizing Your Knowledge

These questions are designed to stimulate critical thinking applications by blending what you've learned in this chapter with everyday applications. For answers to these questions, please refer to Appendix C: Thinking Outside the Box Questions, beginning on page 215.

1. Spend an hour with a companion interacting silently at a shopping mall, in between classes, or at a gathering that includes both acquaintances and non-acquaintances. Do not warn anyone beforehand that you will only be communicating nonverbally. Use all the tools of communication at your disposal to continue sending and receiving messages. How long did this activity continue until someone asked you why you were not speaking? What were some of the difficulties you encountered in attempting to send and receive your messages nonverbally? Which nonverbal strategies were most successful? Which were least successful? Why? If you were to do this activity over again, what would you do differently?

2. With an observer documenting others' reactions, change your pattern of proxemics. Deliberately use the "wrong space" in an elevator, while asking for directions, in conveying affection and personal information with another, and while seated on a bus or train or a lunch room environment. Be as subtle and as natural as possible. Have the observer note each reaction you receive. After each experiment inform the others involved of your experiment and record their feedback: How did your use of the "wrong space" affect them? How did they feel? What judgments or conclusions did they draw about you as a result?

3. Send three messages via mediated communication. The content in each should be identical. In the first use expressive nonverbal tools to indicate sarcasm, in the second use expressive nonverbal tools to indicate disapproval and harshness, and in the third do the same to communicate admiration and affection. Note the variety and creativeness of the ways you attempt to attach different meanings to the same words. What reactions do you receive? Wait an appropriate period of time and then contact the recipients and explain your classroom experiment. Document their second series of reactions.

Online Activities

1. Watch the first fifteen minutes of the movie "Wall-E." Very few words are used, yet numerous emotions are conveyed via nonverbal techniques. How does the title character communicate? Identify the nonverbal functions he performs and the meanings attached.

2. Nonverbal signals are vital to managing our identity. The Will Smith movie "Hitch" typifies the ease with which we can spot the flaws in others and the challenges we encounter in trying to correct our own nonverbal behavior. Identify the nonverbal changes Alex Hitch (Will Smith's character) recommends to Albert (played by Kevin James) and then list the errors committed by Hitch in his pursuit of Sara (the Eva Mendes character).

3. Consult at least three online sources for tips and recommendations on how to use nonverbal communication in job interviews. Do some of the guidelines overlap? Compile a list of "Top Ten Do's" and compare your list with one made by a classmate. Recall and share your own experiences. Can this list of "Top Ten Do's" be of use to you in the future?

Name: _____

Date: _____

Chapter 6: Worksheet #1

1. Define nonverbal communication.

2. Identify seven functions of nonverbal communication.

3. Nonverbal communication differs from verbal communication. Explain, with examples, how they differ in complexity, flow, clarity, impact, and intentionality.

4. What tools of nonverbal communication are on display when members of a class are taking a test?

5. Define proxemics.

(To download this worksheet as a Word document, visit the companion website at www.oup.com/us/adler.)

Name: _____
Date: _____

Chapter 6: Worksheet #2

1. Identify seven tools used to send nonverbal messages.

2. What are the advantages of using touch as a communication tool? What are the disadvantages?

3. Describe three ways you alter your clothing to send messages.

4. Define affect blends and provide two examples.

(To download this worksheet as a Word document, visit the companion website at www.oup.com/us/adler.)

Chapter 7
Understanding Interpersonal Communication

Chapter 7: Mind Map Template

To read the guide to using this mind map and see an example, refer to page 18 of the manual.

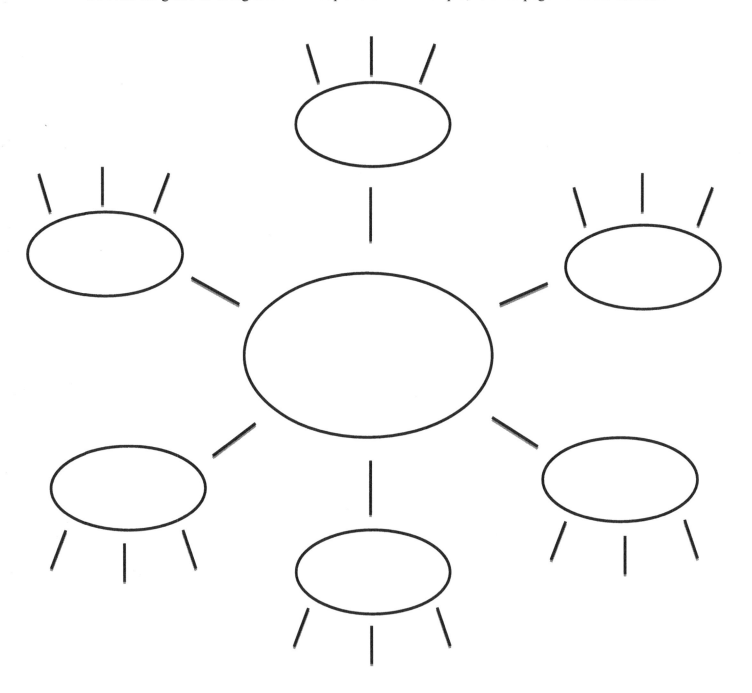

Chapter 7: Outline

Fill in the blank with a key glossary term from the word bank provided. For a completed outline, please refer to the Appendix A: Chapter Outlines, beginning on page 165.

I. Factors influencing our choice of relational partners include superficial as well as contemplative reasons.
   A. Appearance, similarity, complementary characteristics, and reciprocal attraction affect our relationship choices.
   B. We favor individuals we deem capable of competence and use _____ to build liking.
   C. In many cases relationships form due to proximity and the social exchange theory of costs versus rewards.

II. All dyadic communication is _____ _____ _____ _____.
   A. _____ _____ _____ occurs when people treat one another as unique individuals.
   B. Impersonal communication is the opposite, peripheral and fleetingly superficial.
   C. While mediated communication reduces the frequency and quality of face-to-face interaction, it is used by some to enhance the quantity and quality of interpersonal communication. The social support and asynchronous nature of mediated communication contribute to an easy, anonymous courage, resulting in greater self-disclosure.

III. Virtually every verbal statement contains two kinds of messages.
   A. _____ _____ focus on the subject being discussed.
   B. _____ _____ express feelings and attitudes.
   C. The dimensions of relational communications include _____, _____, _____, and _____.
   D. _____ is a term used to describe messages that refer to other messages.

IV. A _____ _____ of the rise and fall of relationships contains phrases of coming together and coming apart.
   A. Coming together is indicated by initiating, experimenting, intensifying, integrating, and bonding.
   B. Differentiating starts the process of coming apart, followed by circumscribing, stagnating, avoiding, and terminating.
   C. Not all relationships follow all the progressive steps, and they usually are fluid and transitory between the stages.

V. Seeking important but often incompatible goals in a relationship results in a
_____ _____ that demonstrates the creation of _____
_____.

    A. These tensions include a connection–autonomy dialectic, a predictability–novelty dialectic, and an openness–privacy dialectic that requires agile juggling.

    B. Managing these dialectical tensions requires the strategy of recognizing denial, overcoming disorientation, using a selection process for the alteration between one end or the other, compartmentalizing different areas in a segmentation tactic, using moderation or compromise to handle the tension, and reframing that could result in reaffirmation.

VI. Even the closest relationships involve a mixture of alternating "we" with "me."

    A. _____ is defined as a close union, contact, association, or acquaintance.

    B. Physical closeness, intellectual sharing, emotion involving an exchange of important feeling, and shared activities provide various states of intimacy.

    C. Women appear more willing to share their thoughts and feelings, and cherish personal talk. Men grow close to one another by doing things together. Generally speaking, men value doing for or with as intimacy.

    D. Personal preferences influence intimacy styles more than gender. People typically orient to either words of affirmation, quality time, acts of service, gifts, or physical touch.

    E. Cultural variances affect how much intimacy is desired.

VII. The process of deliberately revealing information about oneself that is significant and that would not normally be known is called self-disclosure.

    A. The _____ _____ _____ has as its first dimension the _____ of information volunteered. This includes the range of subjects discussed. The second dimension is the _____ of shifting from non-revealing to personal messages.

    B. Another model of self-disclosure is reflected in the _____ _____, where your likes and dislikes, goals, secrets, and needs are then divided into a part you know about and the part you don't know about imposed one atop the other with things others know about you and things you want to keep to yourself. There is an open area and a blind area, a hidden area and an unknown area, and items move from one area to the other through self-disclosure.

    C. Self-disclosure is influenced by culture and usually occurs in dyads. It is usually symmetrical and occurs incrementally. While relatively scarce, self-disclosure uses the guidelines of: is the person important to you, is the risk reasonable, is it appropriate, will it be reciprocated, and is it constructive, clear, and understandable?

VIII. Three common alternatives to self-disclosure are lies, equivocation, and hinting.

A. _____ _____ are defined as intended to be harmless or even helpful. Yet the discovery of lies causes feelings of dismay and betrayal.

B. Equivocation has perceived value as a balance between harsh truths and lying.

C. Hints are more direct than _____ _____ but depend on the other person's ability to pick up the unexpressed message.

Word Bank

affinity	altruistic lies
breadth	content messages
contextually interpersonal communication	control
depth	developmental models
dialectical model	dialectical tensions
equivocal language	immediacy
intimacy	Johari Window
metacommunication	qualitatively interpersonal communication
relational message	respect
self-disclosure	social penetration model

Key Glossary Terms

For each of these terms, define the term, give an example, and explain the significance of the term.

affinity	altruistic lies
breadth	content messages
contextually interpersonal communication	control
depth	developmental models
dialectical model	dialectical tensions
equivocal language	immediacy
intimacy	Johari Window
metacommunication	qualitatively interpersonal communication
relational message	respect
self-disclosure	social penetration model

Chapter 7: Review Questions
These questions are designed to help you understand this chapter's concepts and express your understanding in your own words. For practice with more questions use the course website at www.oup.com/us/adler. For answers to these questions, please refer to Appendix B: Review Questions, beginning on page 194.

1. Identify eight factors shape interpersonal attraction.

2. Diagram and label the developmental stages of the rise and fall of relationships.

3. What are the three competing dialectical tensions in interpersonal relationships?

4. Define the strategies used to distinguish between interpersonal and impersonal relationships.

5. Define content messages.

6. What elements make up the dimensions of a relational message?

7. Define metacommunication and provide three examples.

8. What are the types of intimacy?

9. Identify the guidelines for appropriate self-disclosure.

10. Is there such a thing as a "good lie"? Explain your answer.

Chapter 7: Thinking Outside the Box: Synthesizing Your Knowledge.

These questions are designed to stimulate critical thinking applications by blending what you've learned in this chapter with everyday applications. For answers to these questions, please refer to Appendix C; Thinking Outside the Box Questions, beginning on page 215.

1. Remember your closest and most intimate friend from childhood. What is your relationship with that same person today? Using the stages of relationships as modeled in Figure 7-1, identify the flow in your current status with this person. Provide "for instances."

2. Answer the Self-Assessment of Your Love Languages in Chapter 7. Analyze your responses and explain why you agree or disagree with this assessment.

3. Make an effort to cross the boundary from an impersonal communication exchange to an interpersonal relationship with a casual acquaintance at the grocery store, a boutique in a mall, the lunch counter, or at work. Document the process and whether you succeeded.

4. As an experiment with family and close friends, challenge the guidelines for appropriate self-disclosure. Record the other person's reaction and then reveal your experiment. What was the follow-up response from the other person?

Online Activities

1. Make a list of what you consider the ten best traits in a friend. View the two or three online dating sites and identify the ten most important criteria listed for finding a partner. Now search two or three "Employers seeking" websites and list the top ten skills and values sought by employers. Compare the three lists. Are there similarities? Differences?

2. Look at the relationship between Kevin Costner and James Earl Jones in the movie "Field of Dreams." Identify the stages of the Knapp developmental model in their relationship.

3. Find three people who love their job and three people who hate their job. Ask for specifics as to why. What common relationship elements do you see in their replies?

Name: _____

Date: _____

Chapter 7: Worksheet #1

1. Define interpersonal communication.

2. Define content messages.

3. Identify the four ways relational messages express the communicators' feelings and attitudes.

4. What are three dialectical tensions that exist simultaneously in relational communication?

5. Compare and contrast a direct statement versus a face-saving hint. Give two examples.

(To download this worksheet as a Word document, visit the companion website at www.oup.com/us/adler.)

Name: _____
Date: _____

Chapter 7: Worksheet #2

1. Why do you seek out some people for relationships and not others? Identify eight possible factors.

2. Identify four elements or qualities of intimacy and provide an example of each.

3. Pretend you have exciting but very personal news. You pick the exact news, but it has to do with sex. You are bursting to self-disclose to someone. Here are your choices: a grocery store checkout clerk, your father, the person in line behind you at a convenience store, your professor in speech class, three people in the elevator with you, a co-worker, or a friend you have not seen in several weeks but are in contact with via social media. Whom do you choose? Using the characteristics of effective self-disclosure, explain your answer.

(To download this worksheet as a Word document, visit the companion website at www.oup.com/us/adler.)

Chapter 8
Improving Interpersonal Relationships

Chapter 8: Mind Map Template

To read the guide to using this mind map and see an example, refer to page 18 of the manual.

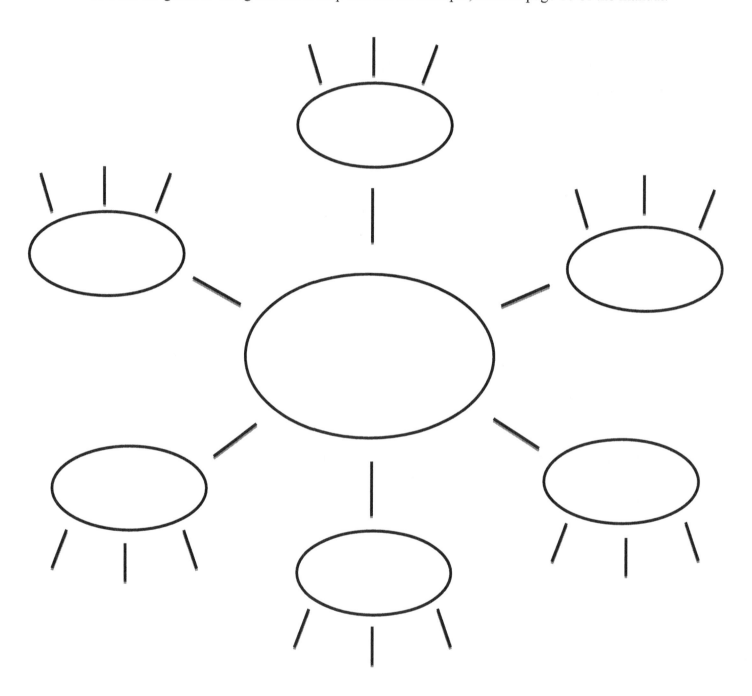

Chapter 8: Outline

Fill in the blank with a key glossary term from the word bank provided. For a completed outline, please refer to the Appendix A: Chapter Outlines, beginning on page 165.

I. Personal relationships are a lot like the weather. The _____ _____ of a relationship refers to the emotional tone involved. The degree to which people see themselves as valued affects the climate.

   A. _____ _____ offer recognition, acknowledgment, and endorsement.

   B. _____ _____ show disagreement, disrespect, disinterest, and negativity.

   C. _____ _____ build from one disconfirming message affecting the climate to a stronger one to an even stronger one to a full-fledged storm! _____ _____ lessen communication through withdrawal, disregard, less investment, and even ignoring the other person involved.

   D. Positive communication climates come about with the ____ _____ of evaluation versus _____, control versus _____ _____, _____versus _____, _____ versus_____, _____ versus _____, and _____ versus_____.

II. Communication _____ is the expressed struggle between at least two interdependent parties who perceive incompatible goals, scarce rewards, and interference from the other parties in achieving their goals.

   A. Conflict is expressed through _____, _____ _____, _____ _____, _____ _____, and assertion.

   B. _____ _____messages are by far the most productive and involve using behavioral descriptions, interpretation of the other's behavior, a description of personal feelings, a description of consequences, and a statement of intention.

   C. Men and women approach conflict differently, with men thriving on competition and women gravitating toward emotional connections.

   D. Cultural variances offer differences in dealing with conflict such as individualistic goals versus collectivist concerns.

III. Every conflict is a struggle, to which there are four possible outcomes: ____-____, ____-____, _____, or ____-____.

   A. Win-Win satisfies the needs of everyone involved. The steps to achieving Win-Win are: identify your problem and unmet needs, make a date, describe your problem and needs, partner check back, solicit partner's needs, check understanding of partner's needs, and negotiate a solution.

B. Steps to negotiation are: identify and define the conflict, generate a number of possible solutions, evaluate the alternative solutions, decide on the best solution, and follow up.

Word Bank

assertive communication	avoidance spiral
certainty	communication climate
compromise	confirming responses
conflict	description
direct aggression	disconfirming responses
empathy	equality
escalatory spiral	Gibb categories
indirect communication	lose-lose
neutrality	nonassertion
passive aggression	problem orientation
provisionalism	spontaneity
strategy	superiority
win-lose	win-win

Key Glossary Terms

For each of these terms, define the term, give an example, and explain the significance of the term.

assertive communication	avoidance spiral
certainty	communication climate
compromise	confirming responses
conflict	controlling communication
description	direct aggression
disconfirming responses	empathy
equality	escalatory spiral
evaluative communication	Gibb categories
"I" language	indirect communication
lose-lose problem solving	neutrality
nonassertion	passive aggression
problem orientation	provisionalism
spiral	spontaneity
strategy	superiority
win-lose problem solving	win-win problem solving
"you" language	

Chapter 8: Review Questions

These questions are designed to help you understand this chapter's concepts and express your understanding in your own words. For practice with more questions use the course website at www.oup.com/us/adler. For answers to these questions, please refer to Appendix B: Review Questions, beginning on page 194.

1. Define communication climate.

2. The quality of our relationships influences the quality of our lives. What are the benefits of healthy relationships and what are the downsides of a poor emotional tone in relationships?

3. Explain confirming messages and contrast them to disconfirming messages.

4. Define communication conflict.

5. Identify five responses to conflict and provide an example of each.

6. Men and women typically approach communication conflict differently. Give examples.

7. Briefly define individualistic versus collectivist cultures and high-context versus low-context communication choices.

8. Why is Win-Win the best outcome to satisfy the needs of everyone involved? Explain your answer by comparing this outcome to other choices. When is compromise justified?

Chapter 8: Thinking Outside the Box: Synthesizing Your Knowledge.

These questions are designed to stimulate critical thinking applications by blending what you've learned in this chapter with everyday applications. For answers to these questions, please refer to Appendix C: Thinking Outside the Box Questions, beginning on page 215.

1. Take the Self-Assessment evaluation "How Assertive Are You?" on page 254 in Chapter 8. Be honest in your replies. What is your assertiveness level? What improvements could you make?

2. Do the Constructing Supportive Messages exercise at the conclusion of Chapter 8. Begin by recalling two situations in which you found yourself in an escalating conflict spiral. Use the Gibb categories to identify your defense-arousing messages, both verbal and nonverbal. Now reconstruct the situations, writing a script in which you replace the defense-arousing behaviors with supportive alternatives. Could the conflict have turned out differently? Clarify your choices.

3. Listen to conversations and communications around you. How often do you detect "you" language? Cite the first five examples and then reword each conversation using "I" language. What differences do you notice?

Online Activities

1. The next time someone resorts to insults, "flaming," bullying, and direct confrontation language via social media, address the person involved using the five steps of a complete assertive message. Before hitting "send" be sure to review the cautionary points from Chapter 8 and the characteristics of an assertive message. What response did you receive?

2. Watch the movie "It Happened One Night." Clark Gable and Claudette Colbert engage in various communication conflicts. Listen for examples of the Gibb categories. Then watch "Think Like a Man." This movie uses both gender and culture in communication conflicts. Note the stereotypical expectations leading to frustrations and escalatory conflict spirals.

Name: _____
Date: _____

Chapter 8: Worksheet #1

1. Identify the three increasingly positive levels of confirming messages.

2. What steps should you follow in negotiating a solution to a communication conflict?

3. You are babysitting your precocious and rambunctious six-year-old nephew. You have a friend with you. You are trying to explain a discipline issue to the child and your friend repeatedly interrupts, takes the child's side of the issue, and corrects your approach and attitude.

   a) Deliver your response with direct aggression.

   b) Detail your assertive response.

*(**To download this worksheet as a Word document, visit the companion website at** www.oup.com/us/adler.)*

Name: _____

Date: _____

Chapter 8: Worksheet #2

1. The characteristics of mediated communication change the nature and approach to communication conflict. Compare and contrast the benefits with the disadvantages of these characteristics.

2. When trying to buy a car, compromise does not mean "meet me halfway." Explain.

3. Passive-aggressive responses to conflict sometimes aggravate the situation more so than direct aggression. Identify at least three traits that reflect hostility in an obscure way.

(To download this worksheet as a Word document, visit the companion website at www.oup.com/us/adler.)

Chapter 9
Communicating in Groups and Teams

Chapter 9: Mind Map Template

To read the guide to using this mind map and see an example, refer to page 18 of the manual.

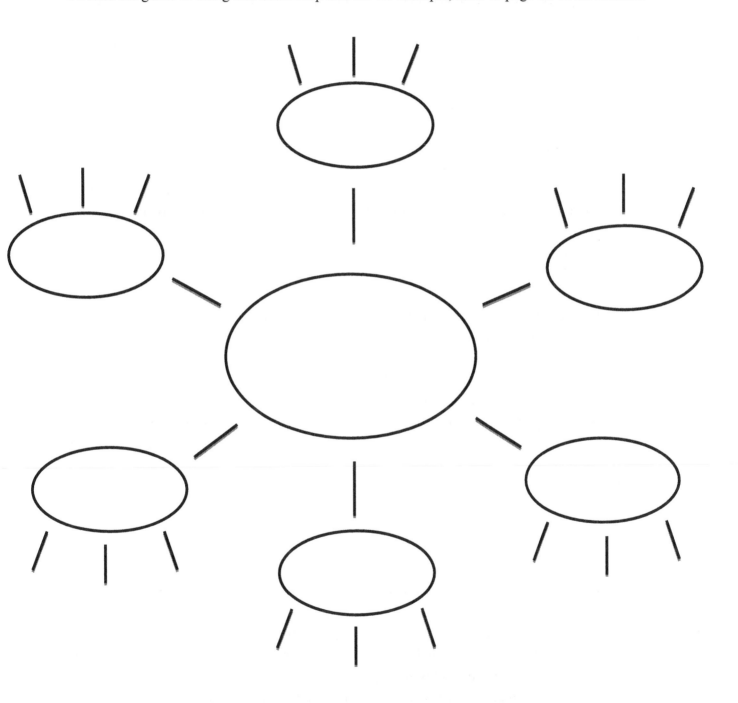

Chapter 9: Outline

Fill in the blank with a key glossary term from the word bank provided. For a completed outline, please refer to the Appendix A: Chapter Outlines, beginning on page 165.

I. A _____ consists of a small collection of people who interact with each other, over time, in order to reach goals.

    A. A team is a group but members work together on a higher level. Teams share clear and inspiring goals, a results-driven structure, competent team members, unified commitment, a collaborative climate, standards of excellence, external support and recognition, and principled leadership.

    B. _____ _____ are teams who interact with one another through mediated communication, without meeting face to face. This form of interaction has advantages in terms of ease and expediency of overcoming geographical challenges and leveling the status differences of rank, age, and gender.

II. Two forces drive group communication: (1) _____ _____, which are the outcomes you seek to accomplish together, and (2) _____ _____, the personal motives of each member.

    A. Most groups meet to achieve a collective task, but social goals of fraternization are equally important.

    B. Individuals participate in groups for many personal reasons; these can become disruptive if the goal consists of a _____ _____, because it is often in conflict with the group goals.

III. All groups and teams have rules and all groups have norms.

    A. A _____ is the official guideline.

    B. _____ are the unspoken standards. _____ ____ govern how members relate and _____ _____ are for operations. ____ ____ govern how members get the job done.

IV. The more complex the structure of groups, the greater effect this has on the flow of information.

    A. ____-_____ _____ allow group members to share the same information. In a _____ _____ information moves sequentially. In a _____ _____, clearinghouse_____ are used to disperse information.

    B. Patterns of behavior by members within the group or team are called_____. _____ ____ are assigned and designated. _____ _____ serve functions but are rarely acknowledged by the group in words. Informal roles fall into two categories:____ help and _____ ____, Other roles are used for maintenance, to continue the relationships and _____ _____, which are unfortunately too common in groups or teams, prevent the group from being effective.

C. Three role-related problems occur when (1) important informal roles go unfilled, (2) competition causes divisiveness, or (3) one member becomes a victim of role fixation (acting out a role whether or not the situation requires it).

V. All groups or teams have a leader or leaders.

A. The _____ _____ _____ relies on legitimate, coercive, and reward power to influence others. In the _____ _____ _____ members share in the decision making. In the _____-_____ _____ _____ the leader relinquishes the power and leaves the group rudderless. A _____ _____ _____ changes with the circumstances.

B. Transactional operators are motivated primarily by personal glory. Team players work to keep members happy and to maintain harmony. Transformational leaders respect the power of teamwork and encourage positive morale.

C. Even in groups that begin with no official leaders, a member or members will become the _____ _____.

VI. If every group or team has a leader then there must be followers.

A. Isolates are indifferent and communicate little outside their environment. Bystanders tend to hang back and watch. Participants attempt to have an impact. Activists are more engaged and passionate. Diehards will, literally, sacrifice themselves for the cause.

B. Followers hold the _____. This ability to influence others has many guises. _____ _____ arises from the title or position one holds. _____ _____ comes from knowledge and competence. _____ _____exists when a member has the ability to develop relationships that help the group. _____ _____is gained by granting or promising a pay-off. _____ _____ involves threats, intimidation, and punishment.

C. _____ _____ comes from the respect, liking, and trust of others.

D. Power is group centered. A leader only has the power granted by the group. Power is distributed among group members and occurs in degrees; it is not an either-or concept.

112

Word Bank

all-channel network	authoritarian leadership style	chain network	coercive power
connection power	democratic leadership style	dysfunctional roles	emergent leader
expert power	formal role	gatekeepers	group
group goals	hidden agendas	individual goals	informal roles
laissez-faire leadership style	legitimate power	norms	power
procedural norms	referent power	reward power	roles
rule	situational leadership	social norms	social roles
task norms	task roles	virtual groups	wheel network

Key Glossary Terms

For each of these terms, define the term, give an example, and explain the significance of the term.

all-channel network	authoritarian leadership style
chain network	coercive power
connection power	democratic leadership style
dysfunctional roles	emergent leader
expert power	formal role
gatekeepers	group
group goals	hidden agendas
individual goals	informal roles
laissez-faire leadership style	Leadership Grid
legitimate power	nominal leader
norms	power
procedural norms	referent power
reward power	roles
rule	situational leadership
social norms	social roles
sociogram	task norms
task roles	trait theories of leadership
virtual groups	wheel network

Chapter 9: Review Questions

These questions are designed to help you understand this chapter's concepts and express your understanding in your own words. For practice with more questions use the course website at www.oup.com/us/adler. For answers to these questions, please refer to Appendix B: Review Questions, beginning on page 194.

1. What characteristics distinguish a group or team from a gathering of people?

2. Two forces drive group communication: group goals and individual goals. What is the difference?

3. Define rules. How do they differ from norms?

4. Group interaction follows a pattern. What are the differences between an all-channel network, a chain network, and a wheel network?

5. Roles define patterns of behaviors in a group or team. Select a group or team of which you are a member and identify the formal roles.

6. Give an example for each of the leadership styles identified in Chapter 9.

7. If there is a leader or leaders there must be followers. Identify the types of followers described in the text.

8. Followers grant power. If there is no one to influence, then leaders are powerless. Starting with "legitimate," identify the many forms of power and cite an example of each.

Chapter 9: Thinking Outside the Box: Synthesizing Your Knowledge.

These questions are designed to stimulate critical thinking applications by blending what you've learned in this chapter with everyday applications. For answers to these questions, please refer to Appendix C: Thinking Outside the Box Questions, beginning on page 215.

1. Take the Self-Assessment of Your Leadership Approach in Chapter 9. Which orientation best describes you? Now take the Self-Assessment on How Good a Follower Are You. Where is your comfort zone? Are you more comfortable being a leader or a follower?

2. Make a list of three groups or teams to which you belong. Identify three rules per group or team and three norms. Do the same rules appear in a different group? How did you acquire the knowledge of the norms?

3. Create a spontaneous game of "Follow the Leader." In the school cafeteria, in a shopping mall, at the end of class, or after a church activity suddenly shout, "Let's play Follow the Leader!" Gather up six or seven or eight intrepid volunteers and ask, "Who wants to be the leader? Go!" Observe the approach to command of the "leader" and the willingness of the followers to award power to the "leader." After two minutes exclaim "New leader! Who wants it? Go!" and watch the process start anew.

Online Activities

1. Go to YouTube and watch the following clips in this order. "Clown Council Meeting" depicts a leader not leading but rather arguing. What would you have done differently? "Bad Leader movie" highlights the traits of bad leadership. Have you experienced any of those leaders? "First Follower: Leadership Lessons from Dancing Guy" clarifies how important followers are for there to be an effective leader.

2. The 1997 version of the movie "12 Angry Men" explores group dynamics in leaders and followers. The group operates with specific rules, but cultural norms hamper effective progress. Note the leadership style used and the types of followers involved.

Name: _____

Date: _____

Chapter 9: Worksheet #1

1. Define a group.

2. List five ways to encourage effective participation in virtual groups.

3. Identify the five traits of an emergent leader.

4. On a scale of 1 to 5 (with 1 being poor and 5 being awesome) rank the productivity and effectiveness of the types of followers.

(To download this worksheet as a Word document, visit the companion website at www.oup.com/us/adler.)

Name: _____
Date: _____

Chapter 9: Worksheet #2

1. Define social norms, procedural norms, and task norms.

2. Give an example of the authoritarian leadership style, democratic leadership style, and laissez-faire leadership style.

3. Define power.

4. a) The coach of the football team has what type of power?

   b) The manager promising a bonus to the top sales-generating staff member of the week is exercising what type of power?

   c) A parent telling a child to go to sleep or get a spanking demonstrates what type of power?

   d) A member of the Art Appreciation Club with an aunt who is curator at the Museum of Modern Art has what type of power?

   e) A candidate for president supported by thousands of followers has what type of power?

(To download this worksheet as a Word document, visit the companion website at www.oup.com/us/adler.)

Chapter 10
Solving Problems in Groups and Teams

Chapter 10: Mind Map Template

To read the guide to using this mind map and see an example, refer to page 18 of the manual.

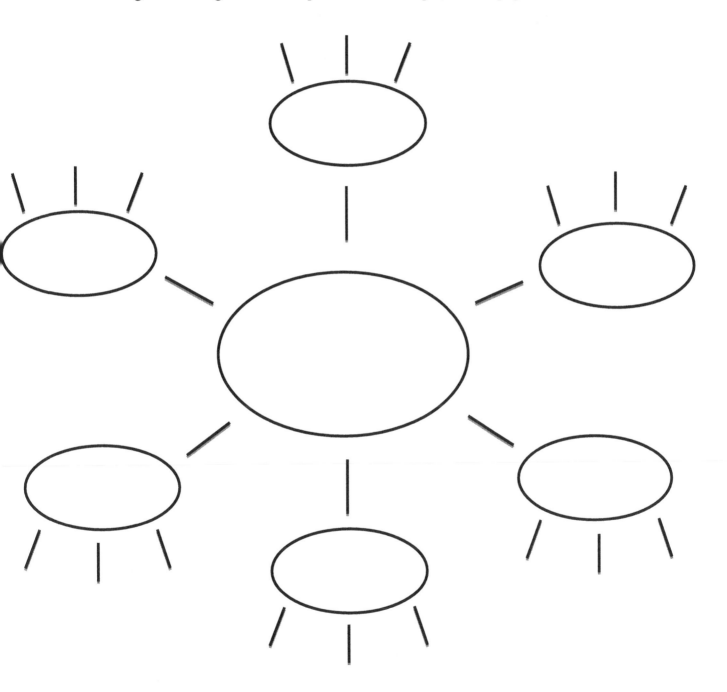

Chapter 10: Outline

Fill in the blank with a key glossary term from the word bank provided. For a completed outline, please refer to the Appendix A: Chapter Outlines, beginning on page 165.

I. In most cases groups can produce more solutions to a problem than individuals.
    A. Problem-solving groups are more effective because they have more resources, an improved rate of accuracy, more commitment, and increased diversity.
    B. Groups are justified if the job is beyond the capacity of one person, if individual tasks are interdependent, if there is more than one possible decision or solution, and if there is potential for disagreement.
II. Groups are most effective when members feel good about one another.
    A. _____, the degree to which members feel connected with and committed to the group, helps a group to be effective.
    B. Cohesiveness is boosted when there are shared or compatible goals, progress toward those goals, and shared norms and values.
    C. Other contributors to cohesiveness are the lack of perceived threat between members, interdependence of members, and a perceived threat outside the group.
    D. Two other components of cohesiveness are the feelings of mutual attraction and friendship and shared group experiences.
III. Many problem-solving groups develop along predictable stages when organizing and strategizing.
    A. Members approach the initial _____ _____ quite tentatively. Once the reason for the group is identified there is a _____ _____ of positions and viewpoints. Give-and-take discussions should progress to a sense of unity and cooperation; thus, the _____ _____ develops as the members become a group. Once the group works together the members support and defend each other in the _____ _____.
    B. Problem-solving groups use a number of formats and approaches to present their results. _____ _____ are offshoots of a larger group, _____ ____ approaches might be used to make a list of ideas to discuss. A _____ _____does not decide the outcome but rather provides solicited feedback.
    C. _____ _____ provides specific rules for discussion and decision making. A _____ _____ involves roundtable contributions with audience members observing and eavesdropping. A _____ presentation occurs when the members divide the topic and each delivers information uninterrupted. _____ groups encourage input and participation from nonmembers. _____ encourages give-and-take and listening to others without superiority with a goal toward understanding.

IV. Often emotions hamper rational differences of opinion in a group, so a template for reflective thinking and decision making is useful.

   A. A structured approach for a problem-solving group would be to identify the problem, analyze the problem, develop creative solutions, evaluate possible solutions, implement the plan, and follow up on the solution.

   B. The decision-making process has several options. Majority control allows quick votes but could exclude 49% of the members. Expert opinion works well if someone has the knowledge but stumbles if not everyone accepts the expert. Minority control has a few decide for the many but overlooks the input of the many. Authority rule is autocratic, efficient, and, at times, dictatorial, but failure to consult members can leave them feeling ordered rather than asked. _____ means all members agree on the decision. The problem there is that full and complete agreement is very difficult to achieve without compromise.

V. Even groups with the best intentions encounter stumbling blocks to effectiveness.

   A. _____ _____, the scarcity of accurate and current input, hinders good results. _____ _____ can overwhelm group members by causing complications and distractions. Unequal participation is the bane of all experienced group members. Unfair balance of responsibilities, a reluctant or absent member, a dysfunctional member demonstrating lack of cooperation: these bog down progress and stifle results.

   B. A strong tendency to "go along to get along," the pressure to conform, often overwhelms dissent when a contrary perspective could be useful.

Word Bank

dialogue	breakout groups
cohesiveness	consensus
conflict stage	emergence stage
focus group	forum
information overload	information underload
orientation stage	panel discussion
parliamentary procedure	problem census
reinforcement stage	symposium

Key Glossary Terms

For each of these terms, define the term, give an example, and explain the significance of the term.

dialogue	brainstorming
breakout groups	cohesiveness
consensus	conflict stage
emergence stage	focus group
force field analysis	forum
groupthink	information overload
information underload	nominal group techniques
orientation stage	panel discussion
parliamentary procedure	participative decision making
problem census	reinforcement stage
symposium	

Chapter 10: Review Questions

These questions are designed to help you understand this chapter's concepts and express your understanding in your own words. For practice with more questions use the course website at www.oup.com/us/adler. For answers to these questions, please refer to Appendix B: Review Questions, beginning on page 194.

1. What can you get from a group that you do not get from an individual?

2. When is a problem-solving group justified?

3. Define cohesiveness and identify the eight factors that can contribute to productivity through cohesiveness.

4. Problem-solving groups use many formats and delivery methods. Describe breakout groups, problem census groups, and focus groups.

5. Identify the differences between panel discussion, symposium, forum, and dialogue problem solving.

6. Outline the working format for progressing from identifying a problem to following up on the solution.

7. What are the advantages and disadvantages of group decision-making choices?

8. The most common complaint in group assignments is unequal participation of members. How can this be avoided?

Chapter 10: Thinking Outside the Box: Synthesizing Your Knowledge

These questions are designed to stimulate critical thinking applications by blending what you've learned in this chapter with everyday applications. For answers to these questions, please refer to Appendix C: Thinking Outside the Box Questions, beginning on page 215.

1. Take the Chapter 10 Self-Assessment on How Effective Is Your Team. Analyze your results. What did you discover about the team effectiveness? What obvious steps could be taken to alter your score?

2. Over the course of a week's time observe instances of the many decision-making methods in action. Document the circumstances and the problem being solved. For example: the professor deciding when class begins or ends, a customer service counter at a retail store handling a return, a jury verdict, a city council meeting, etc. Identify the method and any observations you have regarding the pros and cons of the decision. How might you have done things differently?

3. Have you ever moved and had assistance? Has a friend ever used you to help move? Describe the problem-solving process involved in moving.

Online Activities

1. Write a mystery story! Form an online team of at least three friends. Establish rules and norms: Violence allowed? How graphic? Sex? How graphic? Realism or fantasy? Modern era or in another age? Can each participating author insert new characters or plot twists? Is this a turn-taking exercise or can anyone contribute anything at any time? One page from each or one paragraph? Multiple pages or concepts or only one? Are plot twists from movies or literature allowed? How will responsibility be divided?

Establish the parameters. Set a timeline and a due date (perhaps one or two weeks max). Then start about tackling the challenge.

Here is the opening line….

> *"Verna Chang knew something was wrong, bad wrong, the moment she saw the dog limping from the opening of the cave."*

Let the creativity commence.

Once the project is complete, survey the multiple co-authors on the effectiveness of the team effort.

2. Establish a "What are we going to do about_____?" group online. Select a topic of interest to your invited members. It does not have to be political or of dramatic social significance; the object is to have an attainable, reasonable, realistic outcome. "What are we going to do about the high cost of textbooks?" "What are we going to do about food choices on campus?" "What are we going to do about recreation options in the nearby area?" Share the brainstorming strategies recommended in the text and the format for problem-solving and see where the problem-solving group goes from there.

Name: _____
Date: _____

Chapter 10: Worksheet #1

1. What are the four advantages of solving a problem via a group and not as an individual?

2. When is it justified to use a group to solve problems?

3. What is the difference between a panel discussion and a forum?

4. Which decision-making process is the strongest, and what are its drawbacks?

5. Define cohesiveness.

(To download this worksheet as a Word document, visit the companion website at www.oup.com/us/adler.)

Name: _____
Date: _____

Chapter 10: Worksheet #2

1. Eight factors contribute to cohesiveness in a group. Identify at least five.

2. What is the first step of a problem-solving group taking a systematic approach to their dilemma?

3. What is the first stage of development for a group? Define that stage.

4. What are the pitfalls and dangers groups must overcome so that progress does not become bogged down?

5. How can you, as a group member, achieve balance in group participation?

(To download this worksheet as a Word document, visit the companion website at www.oup.com/us/adler.)

Chapter 11
Preparing and Presenting Your Speech

Chapter 11: Mind Map Template

To read the guide to using this mind map and see an example, refer to page 18 of the manual.

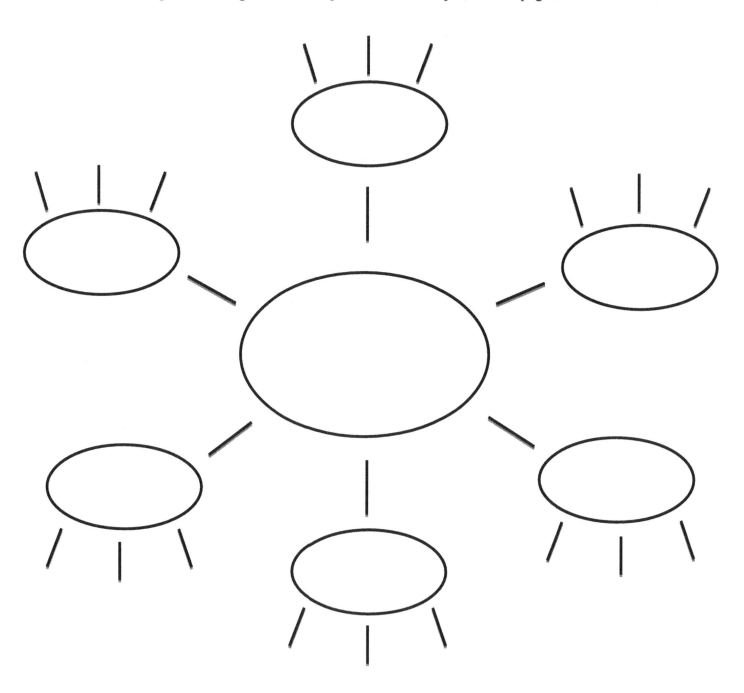

Chapter 11: Outline

Fill in the blank with a key glossary term from the word bank provided. For a completed outline, please refer to the Appendix A: Chapter Outlines, beginning on page 165.

I. The three steps to preparing a speech are: choose a topic, determine your purpose, and find information.
   A. Pick a topic that interests you. Pick a topic early. More time means more research and practice.
   B. The _____ _____ of your speech is expressed in a complete sentence that describes exactly what you want your speech to accomplish. This _____ _____ should stem from your overall _____ _____ to inform, persuade, or entertain.
   C. The purpose statement should be results-oriented, specific, and realistic.
   D. The _____ _____ tells your listeners the general idea.
II. Two things to always consider in preparing a speech: the audience and the occasion.
   A. _____ _____ involves identifying and adapting your remarks to your listeners.
   B. Audience members are there for a reason. You need to know the audience purpose. Characteristics such as age, gender, cultural diversity, group membership, and so on are audience _____. What is the audience _____? What are their _____ and _____?
   C. A second step in preparation takes into account the time, place, and audience expectations.
III. Now you are ready to find information.
   A. Use online research if you can verify its credibility, objectivity, and currency. Is the material accurate and truthful, is it non-biased, and is it recent?
   B. Use library catalog sources, reference works, periodicals,_____, and interviews for accurate information. _____ _____ is another venue to explore for source material and involves distributing questionnaires to peers and other contributors.
IV. You are getting the material ready, so how about the fear of giving a speech?
   A. _____ _____ _____ involves some nervousness and anxiety. That is to be expected. Confidence reinforced by practice and more practice addresses the usual butterflies common to all.
   B. _____ _____ _____ involves panic, the fight-or-flight reflex, and crippling self-doubt. Previous negative experiences, _____ _____, the _____ __ _____ _____ (anticipating that something awful will happen), the _____ __ _____ expected from the listeners, the _____ __ _____ (where you think you have to

please everyone), and the _____ __ _____ (where you blow things totally out of proportion) all contribute to debilitative anxiety.

C. Fight back by using the nervousness to your advantage, understanding the difference between rational concerns and irrational fears, maintaining a receiver orientation (this is for them and not about you), keeping a positive attitude where your _____ is one of success, and being prepared. Practice ahead of time and anticipate all possible challenges.

V. The decision on how to present the speech is your next step of preparation.

A. An _____ _____ is planned in advance and presented in a conversational tone. An _____ _____ is spontaneous and unplanned. A _____ _____ is written out and then read word for word. A _____ _____ is learned and presented without notes.

B. Other delivery considerations include appearance, movement, posture, facial expressions, gestures, and eye contact.

C. Auditory aspects of delivery include volume, ____, _____, word choice, and _____.

D. The four most common articulation challenges are _____, _____, _____, and _____.

Word Bank

addition	articulation
attitude	audience analysis
beliefs	databases
debilitative communication apprehension	deletion
demographics	extemporaneous speech
facilitative communication apprehension	fallacy of approval
fallacy of catastrophic failure	fallacy of overgeneralization
fallacy of perfection	general purpose
impromptu speech	irrational thinking
manuscript speech	memorized speech
pitch	purpose statement

rate

specific purpose

survey research

values

slurring

substitution

thesis statement

visualization

Key Glossary Terms

For each of these terms, define the term, give an example, and explain the significance of the term.

addition

attitude

belief

debilitative communication apprehension

demographics

facilitative communication apprehension

fallacy of catastrophic failure

fallacy of perfection

impromptu speech

manuscript speech

pitch

rate

specific purpose

survey research

value

articulation

audience analysis

database

deletion

extemporaneous speech

fallacy of approval

fallacy of overgeneralization

general purpose

irrational thinking

memorized speech

purpose statement

slurring

substitution

thesis statement

visualization

Chapter 11: Review Questions

These questions are designed to help you understand this chapter's concepts and express your understanding in your own words. For practice with more questions use the course website at www.oup.com/us/adler. For answers to these questions, please refer to Appendix B: Review Questions, beginning on page 194.

1. Name the first three tasks for starting a speech.

2. No one gives a speech without having a reason to do so. What are criteria should the purpose statement of your presentation should meet?

3. Audience analysis involves identifying and adapting your remarks to the most pertinent characteristics of your listeners. What elements are involved in audience demographics?

4. The occasion of a speech is determined by the circumstances surrounding it. Name three of these circumstances.

5. Before using any online sources in your speech, you should gauge and evaluate the material based on three criteria. What are they?

6. Identify five avenues of information available besides online sources.

7. How should a nervous speaker cope with facilitative communication apprehension?

8. Why are people afflicted with debilitative communication apprehension? List six reasons.

9. What is the most common type of delivery for a speech? What are its advantages over the other types?

Chapter 11: Thinking Outside the Box: Synthesizing Your Knowledge

These questions are designed to stimulate critical thinking applications by blending what you've learned in this chapter with everyday applications. For answers to these questions, please refer to Appendix C; Thinking Outside the Box Questions, beginning on page 215.

1. Plan, prepare, and present an "elevator speech." Give a short, presentation of who you are, what you do, and the most admirable assets you possess in the span of 30 seconds to two minutes. The idea is to grab the attention of the listeners and stimulate interest in wanting to know more. It should be a fast-paced, pithy sales pitch about you. Recite it out loud to yourself then try it out on a listener.

2. Recall a television show, movie, or recent personal incident and tell a friend about it. Hold your hands clasped behind your back, do not make eye contact, and do not add vocal inflections to your voice. When you finish, let your friend know you were experimenting with delivery techniques Ask for feedback on your effectiveness in relaying the information.

3. You have been asked to give a speech at an elementary school on "The Benefits of Playing Checkers." What questions would you ask the person arranging the speech?

Online Activities

1. View the YouTube video of "Miss Teen USA 2007 South Carolina answers a question." Could you have given a better impromptu speech? Think so? Okay. Right now, quickly, answer the question that was asked. Impromptu is not so easy, is it! Watch "Introduction Speech Gone Wrong: What Not To Do." Do you now understand the dangers of memorization? Then there is Don Knotts and "Nervous Speech." This was supposed to be a manuscript speech. Because of what happened, can you identify the vocal and visual flaws he committed? And finally watch a prepared speech, "We Choose To Go To The Moon" by John F. Kennedy (the short version works well for demonstration purposes). Notice the visual and vocal aspects even with a manuscript.

2. The movie "The King's Speech" addresses speech apprehension and vocal challenges. You think your self-doubt is overwhelming? Put yourself in the King's shoes.

3. Your speech topic is "The Minimum Wage." Compare and contrast three online sources that meet the guidelines of credibility, objectivity, and currency and three that do not.

Name: _____
Date: _____

Chapter 11: Worksheet #1

1. List the four methods of delivering a speech.

2. Cite sources of debilitative communication apprehension and the antidote to each.

3. What can you control, knowing the audience is listening to you?

4. What is the difference between a purpose statement and a thesis statement?

(To download this worksheet as a Word document, visit the companion website at www.oup.com/us/adler.)

Name: _____
Date: _____

Chapter 11: Worksheet #2

1. Take the Chapter 11 Self-Assessment: Speech Anxiety questionnaire. If your score is under 9 (be honest!), move on to the next question. If it is higher than 9, identify five strategies to help you manage your worries.

2. If your Self-Assessment score was under 9, list three mental tips you would recommend to others. Scored over 9? Consider the concept of more preparation. When are speakers typically the most nervous? Why?

3. Given your choice of presentation delivery methods, which one do you prefer and why?

(To download this worksheet as a Word document, visit the companion website at www.oup.com/us/adler.)

Chapter 12
Organization and Support

Chapter 12: Mind Map Template

To read the guide to using this mind map and see an example, refer to page 18 of the manual.

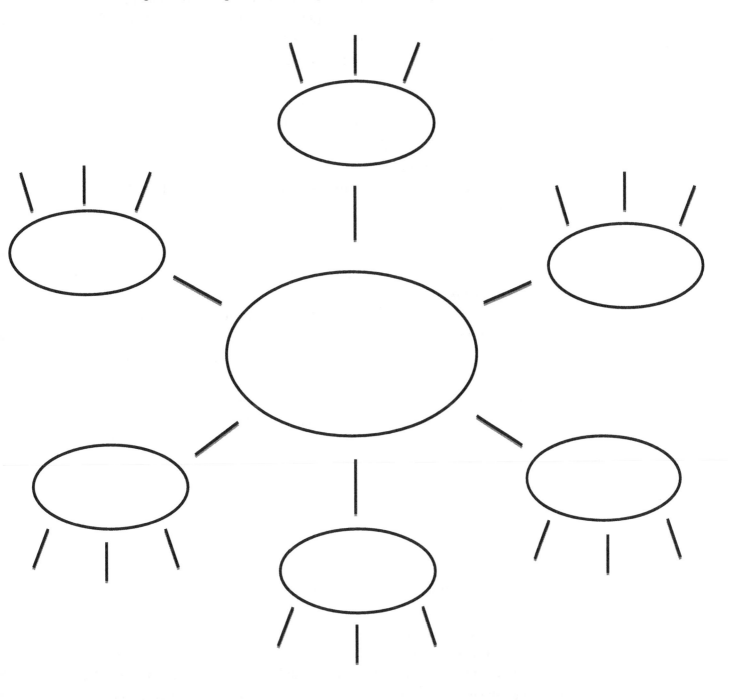

Chapter 12: Outline

Fill in the blank with a key glossary term from the word bank provided. For a completed outline, please refer to the Appendix A: Chapter Outlines, beginning on page 165.

I. Building a speech starts with a strong foundation. The outline is that foundation.
   A. A _____ _____ is a construction tool to map out your speech. This is for your eyes only, informal and rough, used to refine and solidify ideas.
   B. A _____ _____ uses a consistent format and set of symbols.
   C. Speaking notes are used to jog your memory. These are usually brief phrases and keywords organized to aid the flow and progression of the speech.
   D. Following a standard format contributes to neatness, ease of scanning, and coordination of main points and sub-points.
II. The outline must be organized in a logical pattern.
   A. _____ _____ organize things in chronological order: first came this, then this, then lastly this.
   B. _____ _____ are organized according to area: moving from east to west or smaller to larger.
   C. _____ _____ follow types or categories: well-known to less familiar, classifications that progress to the next step or stage.
   D. _____-_____ _____ describe what is wrong and propose a way to make things better. This is a popular format for persuasive speeches.
   E. _____-_____ _____ discuss what happened and then the consequences of what happened.
   F. Monroe's motivated sequence gets attention, addresses a need, offers satisfaction, paints a beneficial visualization, and then calls for action.
III. Moving from one portion or component of the speech to the next is accomplished by using _____.
   A. Transitions help relate one point to the next. They move the flow from highlight to highlight and soothe the hectic stop-start of presenting.
   B. Transitions connect and bond the components of the outline pattern to conversational delivery.
IV. Every speech starts with an _____.
   A. The first goal of an introduction is to capture the attention of the audience. There are many approaches possible, but the most important thing to remember is you want the audience to pay attention.
   B. An effective introduction states the speaker's thesis by previewing main points.
   C. The beginning of your speech sets the mood and tone of the speech. You must demonstrate the importance of your topic to the audience and establish your credibility.

V. Although some anxious speakers have their doubts, every speech has a _____. It will end!

    A. The conclusion should restate the thesis, review main points, and provide a memorable final remark.

    B. Bad conclusions ruin an otherwise good speech, so remember the four "don'ts": don't end abruptly, don't ramble, don't introduce new points, and don't apologize.

VI. Charisma and character do not guarantee the audience's attention unless you have supporting material.

    A. The role of supporting material is to clarify, prove, make interesting, and make memorable.

    B. Various types of supporting material include definition, _____, _____, _____/comparison-contrast, _____, and quotation/_____.

    C. The _____ style of presenting means telling a story or relating an incident. _____ uses someone else's work; you are using it as a statement of fact.

Word Bank

analogy	anecdote
cause-effect pattern	citation
conclusion	example
formal outline	introduction
narration	problem-solution pattern
space pattern	testimony
time pattern	topic pattern
transition	working outline

Key Glossary Terms

For each of these terms, define the term, give an example, and explain the significance of the term.

analogy	anecdote
cause-effect pattern	citation
climax pattern	conclusion
example	formal outline
hypothetical example	introduction
narration	problem-solution pattern
space pattern	testimony
time pattern	topic pattern
transition	working outline

Chapter 12: Review Questions

These questions are designed to help you understand this chapter's concepts and express your understanding in your own words. For practice with more questions use the course website at www.oup.com/us/adler. For answers to these questions, please refer to Appendix B: Review Questions, beginning on page 194.

1. A working outline of a speech is used for what purpose?

2. What purposes are served by using a formal outline when preparing your speech?

3. Identify and define six patterns of logical organization that can be used in outlining a speech.

4. What are the four functions of a speech introduction?

5. Cite four ways to get the attention of the audience in the introduction.

6. You have to establish credibility quickly in your introduction. What are three techniques you can use?

7. The conclusion is not simply the end of the speech; it has three essential functions. Name them.

8. What are the four big "don'ts" of a conclusion?

9. There are four functions of supporting materials. List them.

10. Many types of supporting material are available to fulfill the functions identified in Question #9. Name five.

Chapter 12: Thinking Outside the Box: Synthesizing Your Knowledge

These questions are designed to stimulate critical thinking applications by blending what you've learned in this chapter with everyday applications. For answers to these questions, please refer to Appendix C; Thinking Outside the Box Questions, beginning on page 215.

1. Do the Chapter 12 Self-Assessment: Main Points and Subpoints. How long did it take? If it took longer than 30 seconds, practice again with a different topic. Brainstorm a list of all the concepts involved with "Visiting a relative during a holiday." Now organize the concepts in an outline form similar to one used in the Self-Assessment example. How did you do? Practice again. This time the subject is "Applying for a job you really, really want." And the results? You will get more efficient with practice.

2. Your speech is titled "Jumping out of an Airplane." Create four different opening statements that accomplish the functions of an effective introduction.

3. A bad conclusion destroys an otherwise good book, movie, song, and speech. Recall your past experiences and give an example of each of the major "don'ts" being committed. One example per "don't," please!

Online Activities

1. Go online and find three recipes for green bean casserole. Compile the three by using the outlining recommendations from Chapter 12. Organize and prioritize the main points and subpoints. Insert appropriate accreditation of sources as supporting material. You now have a How-To speech ready to present to an audience.

2. Use the Internet to find the text to these three speeches: (1) Sojourner Truth and "Ain't I A Woman?" (2) Ursula LeGuin and "A Left-Handed Commencement Address" and (3) Oprah Winfrey's "Eulogy for Rosa Parks." Outline these three speeches.

3. Use YouTube and view "The Chili Peppers Speech." List the types of supporting material used in this speech.

Name: _____

Date: _____

Chapter 12: Worksheet #1

1. Create an example of a time pattern outline.

2. What are the five steps of the motivated sequence?

3. List the four functions of an effective speech introduction.

4. Identify four things not to do in the conclusion of the speech.

5. What is an anecdote? Cite one.

(To download this worksheet as a Word document, visit the companion website at www.oup.com/us/adler.)

Name: _____

Date: _____

Chapter 12: Worksheet #2

1. A formal outline serves several purposes. Name three.

2. What is the purpose of transitions?

3. List six ways to get the attention of your listener at the start of your speech.

4. What are the functions of a conclusion?

5. Define narration.

6. Define citation.

7. List five types of supporting material and then rank them on a scale of 1 to 5 (*1 being "meh" and 5 being "wow"*) in terms of their effectiveness in a speech.

(To download this worksheet as a Word document, visit the companion website at www.oup.com/us/adler.)

Chapter 13
Informative Speaking

Chapter 13: Mind Map Template

To read the guide to using this mind map and see an example, refer to page 18 of the manual.

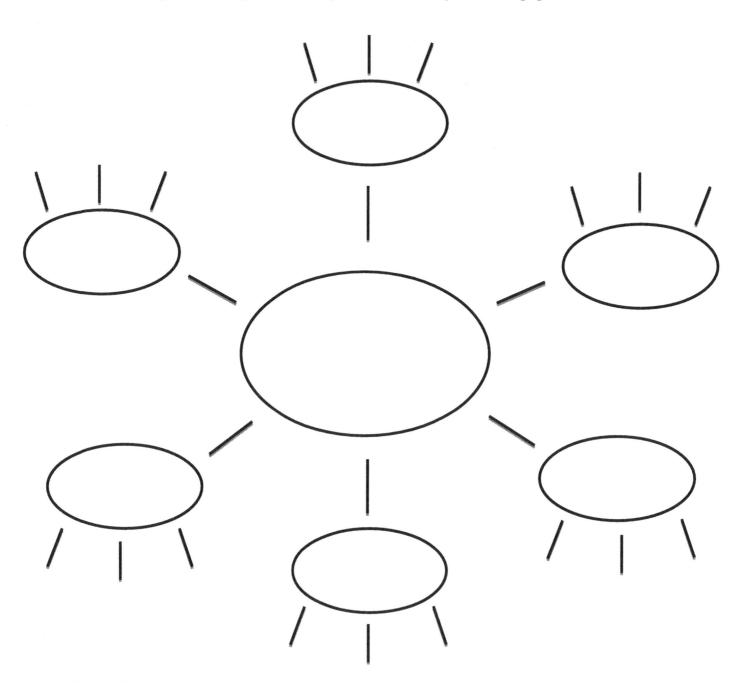

Chapter 13: Outline

Fill in the blank with a key glossary term from the word bank provided. For a completed outline, please refer to the Appendix A: Chapter Outlines, beginning on page 165.

I. There is a lot of information out there, almost too much. How do you cope?
   A. _____ _____ is a form of stress where people get confused and have trouble sorting out the wheat from the chaff.
   B. _____ _____ results in mind clutter and frustration over what to discard and what to turn into _____.
   C. Effective public speakers use information to give knowledge to the listeners.
II. Informative speeches primarily have to do with content and purpose.
   A. Content speeches deal with objects, processes, events, and concepts.
   B. Speeches dealing with purpose involve _____, _____, and _____.
   C. Informative speeches tend to be noncontroversial and do not attempt to change the audience's opinions.
   D. Persuasive speeches advocate change and expect resistance to acceptance.
III. The techniques of informative speaking help an audience understand and care.
   A. Formulate a specific _____ _____ _____. Create _____ _____. Make it easy to listen. Use clear, simple language. Use a clear organization and structure.
   B. It is very beneficial to use supportive material effectively. Emphasize important points. Generate _____ _____ and encourage _____ _____. Use _____ that emphasize upcoming material. Use _____ _____.
   C. There are a wide variety of choices for visual aids, such as objects and _____, _____, _____ _____, _____ _____, ____ _____, ____ _____, _____ _____, ___ _____, chalk and whiteboards, posters and pads, handouts, projectors, power point, Prezi, keynote, video, _____ _____, audio, and physical demonstrations.
   D. Visual aids should be evaluated for simplicity, size, attractiveness, appropriateness, and reliability.

Word Bank

audience involvement	audience participation
bar chart	column chart
description	diagram
explanation	information anxiety
information hunger	information overload
informative purpose statement	instructions
knowledge	line chart
model	number chart
pie chart	signpost
visual aids	word chart

Key Glossary Terms

For each of these terms, define the term, give an example, and explain the significance of the term.

audience involvement	audience participation
bar chart	column chart
description	diagram
explanation	information anxiety
information hunger	information overload
informative purpose statement	instructions
knowledge	line chart
model	number chart
pictogram	pie chart
signpost	visual aids
word chart	

Chapter 13: Review Questions

These questions are designed to help you understand this chapter's concepts and express your understanding in your own words. For practice with more questions use the course website at www.oup.com/us/adler. For answers to these questions, please refer to Appendix B: Review Questions, beginning on page 194.

1. What can you do to overcome information overload and create information hunger for your speech?

2. Speaking clearly and accenting your speech with purposeful nonverbal accompaniment will not suffice unless you make it easy to listen to. How do you do this?

3. What rough outline or plan of action should you map out in structuring an informative speech?

4. Audience involvement is vital. In addition to good delivery via enthusiasm, energy, eye contact, movement, and vocal variety, what other options do you have?

5. List six possible visual aids for a speech and cite the rules for visual aids.

6. Cite three "pros" for using presentation software and three "cons" against it.

7. What are two differences between an informative speech and a persuasive speech?

8. Name two ways to emphasize important points in a speech.

Chapter 13: Thinking Outside the Box: Synthesizing Your Knowledge.

These questions are designed to stimulate critical thinking applications by blending what you've learned in this chapter with everyday applications. For answers to these questions, please refer to Appendix C; Thinking Outside the Box Questions, beginning on page 215.

1. Take the Chapter 13 Self-Assessment: Are You Overloaded With Information? Whatever your score, you should review and employ the techniques in this chapter on how to help your audience listen, creating information hunger, and effective visual aids.

2. Recall a concert, movie, sporting event, television show, or personal incident. Prepare to give an informative speech on this subject to a classmate or friend. Once you organize your informative speech structure, re-examine the Chapter 13 tips on generating audience involvement. List specific ways you can personalize the information, get audience participation, use a volunteer, or have a question-and-answer session during the speech.

3. We have all suffered through overlong, over-complicated, and uninteresting speech presentations. Think back. Were visual aids involved? What went wrong? What would you have done differently?

Online Activities

1. Go to YouTube and view George Carlin's informative speech "I'm a Modern Man."

   a. How does he create information hunger and make it easy to listen? Cite specifics.
   b. Is his language clear and simple? Give examples.
   c. How well does he organize his points? Can you outline this speech? Try it.
   d. Does he emphasize important points? How?
   e. Is there audience involvement? Explain.

2. Go to YouTube and view "Bill Cosby: Dentists."

   a. Was this narration or citation? Explain your answer.
   b. Is this an informative speech of content or purpose? Defend your answer.
   c. Did he create information hunger? How?
   d. Did he fulfill the objectives of an effective introduction?
   e. What visual aids did he use?

3. Pick one of these topics for an informative speech:

   - How to change a flat tire
   - How to accessorize and coordinate from head to toe
   - I want you to meet Martti Ahtisaari.
   - The life and times of Lil Hardin Armstrong
   - It happened in Pompeii.

Do research and list five supporting material choices, including online sources and visual aids, you would use in this speech. Give specifics.

Name: _____
Date: _____

Chapter 13: Worksheet #1

1. How can you put information together in a way that makes it easy to listen? List three ways and give an example for each.

2. In your speech you want everyone to know honey bees will not sting you unless you upset them, honey bees are vital to the growth and continuation of pretty flowers, and the price of honey is increasing because bees are getting scarce. What are two techniques you can use to emphasize these important points? Cite examples.

3. Your speech is titled "What to do to get ready for a job interview." How can you generate audience involvement? Explain.

(To download this worksheet as a Word document, visit the companion website at www.oup.com/us/adler.)

Name: _____
Date: _____

Chapter 13: Worksheet #2

1. State the specific informative purpose statement of Chapter 13.

2. What considerations and rules should you keep in mind when using visual aids?

3. What is the difference between information and knowledge?

4. After reviewing the pros and cons of using presentation software as supporting material in a speech, are you more inclined or less inclined to use it in a speech? Explain your answer.

(To download this worksheet as a Word document, visit the companion website at www.oup.com/us/adler.)

Chapter 14
Persuasive Speaking

Chapter 14: Mind Map Template

To read the guide to using this mind map and see an example, refer to page 18 of the manual.

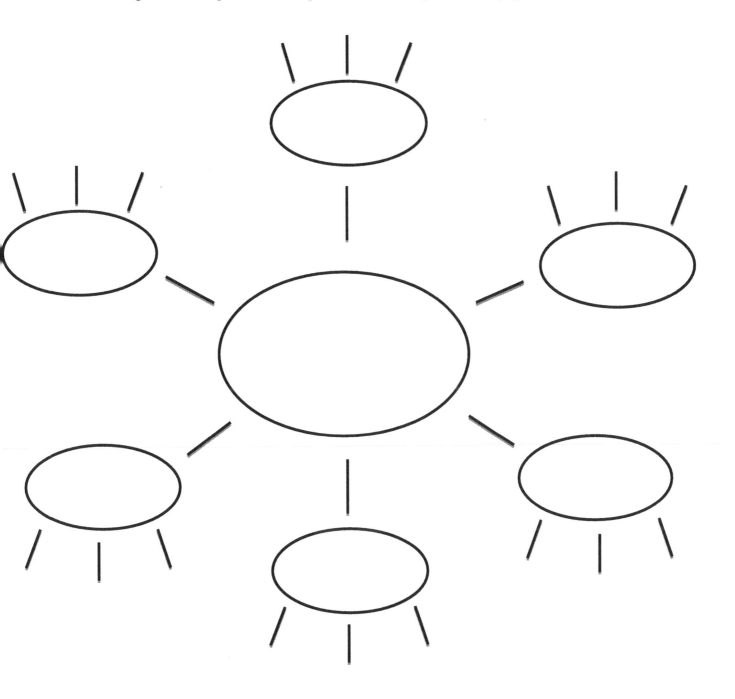

Chapter 14: Outline

Fill in the blank with a key glossary term from the word bank provided. For a completed outline, please refer to the Appendix A: Chapter Outlines, beginning on page 165.

I. _____ is the process of motivating someone, through communication, to change a particular belief, attitude, or behavior.
   A. Persuasion is not coercive but it is usually incremental.
   B. The _____ _____ ____ is used by listeners to compare the opinions of the speaker to ones they already hold.
   C. The preexisting opinion is known as the _____ and any movement or change goes along a diagram of _____ __ _____, _____ __ _____, and _____ __ _____.
   D. Persuasion is interactive. Persuasion differs from coercion in that it is ethical. _____ _____ is communication in the best interest of the audience that does not depend on false or misleading information to change the audience's attitude or behavior.

II. There are several types of persuasion depending on the proposition being advanced.
   A. _____ __ _____ come up when there are two or more sides and the audience is being asked to choose.
   B. _____ __ __ _____ explore the worth of an idea, person, or object.
   C. _____ __ __ _____ recommend a specific course of action.

III. Persuasion offers two possible desired outcomes. _____ the audience to change a way of thinking is one desired outcome. The other is to set about to _____ an audience into a specific behavior.
   A. _____ _____ is used to make the message clear early in the speech.
   B. _____ _____ deemphasizes the purpose to allow a hostile or unfriendly audience time to adjust to the proposal.

IV. Persuasion has been called a "reason-giving discourse." The technique, therefore, of creating a persuasive message involves proposing claims and backing those claims up with accurate reasons.
   A. There must be a clear, persuasive purpose with a message that is structured carefully.
   B. The speaker needs to describe the problem, describe the solution, describe the desired audience response, and then combine the solution with the desired audience response. One recommended way to do this is to use the _____ _____.
   C. Solid _____ is mandatory in persuasion, and this includes _____ _____that evokes feelings.

V. Too often the ethical approach of persuasion is hampered by errors in logic. A _____ of logic can negate any possible movement the listener might have been contemplating.
   A. The __ _____ _____ attacks the person instead of the argument. A _____ __ _____ _____ takes the argument to ridiculous extremes. _____-__ _____ proposals issue ultimatums and set up false alternatives.
   B. Additional logical errors take place when the speaker uses the ____ ___ _____. This mistakenly assumes one event caused another because they happened sequentially. An _____ __ _____ _____ involves relying on the testimony of someone who has a title or fame but is not an expert. Mass appeal is often used via the _____ __ _____ _____, also called bandwagon. Just because many approve does not mean it is the correct decision.
VI. High on the list of priorities for a persuasive speech is the need to appreciate your _____ _____.
   A. Persuasive speakers should establish a common ground and organize according to the expected response.
   B. The speaker needs to neutralize potential hostility and build _____ as a speaker. To have credibility means you are believable.
   C. Competence means expertise on the subject. Character implies trustworthiness, and charisma means likability.
   D. Aristotle referred to these qualities as _____ to mean credibility, _____ to appeal to emotion, and _____ to affect reasoning and logic.

Word Bank

actuate	ad hominem fallacy
anchor	argumentum ad populum fallacy
argumentum ad verecundiam fallacy	convincing
credibility	direct persuasion
either-or fallacy	emotional evidence
ethical persuasion	ethos
evidence	fallacy
indirect persuasion	latitude of acceptance
latitude of noncommitment	latitude of rejection

158

logos

pathos

post hoc fallacy

proposition of policy

reductio ad absurdum fallacy

target audience

motivated sequence

persuasion

proposition of fact

proposition of value

social judgment theory

Key Glossary Terms

For each of these terms, define the term, give an example, and explain the significance of the term.

actuate

anchor

argumentum ad verecundiam fallacy

credibility

either-or fallacy

ethical persuasion

evidence

indirect persuasion

latitude of noncommitment

logos

pathos

post hoc fallacy

proposition of policy

reductio ad absurdum fallacy

target audience

ad hominem fallacy

argumentum ad populum fallacy

convincing

direct persuasion

emotional evidence

ethos

fallacy

latitude of acceptance

latitude of rejection

motivated sequence

persuasion

proposition of fact

proposition of value

social judgment theory

Chapter 14: Review Questions

These questions are designed to help you understand this chapter's concepts and express your understanding in your own words. For practice with more questions use the course website at www.oup.com/us/adler. For answers to these questions, please refer to Appendix B: Review Questions, beginning on page 194.

1. If your persuasive purpose is designed to change the way the audience thinks, the desired outcome is what?

2. You do not have to swing them from one belief or attitude to another to achieve the desired outcome, but you do have to…? Name three objectives.

3. When you want to move the audience to a specific behavior, this is a desired outcome of what?

4. The two types of action you want are…..?

5. To differ from coercion, persuasion must be ethical. Identify five unethical communication behaviors.

6. Define credibility.

7. What are the three "C's" of credibility?

8. Name four components of adapting to your target audience.

9. List the logical fallacies to avoid in a persuasive speech.

10. Your audience is hostile and reluctant to change. What approach do you employ?

11. What are the steps of the motivated sequence?

12. Give some examples of coercion.

Chapter 14: Thinking Outside the Box: Synthesizing Your Knowledge

These questions are designed to stimulate critical thinking applications by blending what you've learned in this chapter with everyday applications. For answers to these questions, please refer to Appendix C; Thinking Outside the Box Questions, beginning on page 215.

1. Watch one hour of network television. Pay particular attention to the commercials; after all, they are miniature persuasive presentations. Make a note of the product advertised and the approach used. Direct or indirect? What is the desired outcome? Do you detect any logical fallacies being committed? Cite the commercial and the fallacy. As an added challenge, how long does it take to experience every logical fallacy mentioned in the text?

2. Select a persuasive topic you are either for or against. Create a questionnaire for your classmates. You do not want to tip your hand as to which side you are taking (not yet), but you do want to know more about your audience. Shape your questions as a way to determine your approach and desired outcome. You will need at least 10 questions. What are they?

3. Do you eat foods now you did not eat as a child? Have your opinions on certain things changed since you were 5 or 6 years old—things like kissing, going to school, immunization shots, or something more social or political? What was your anchor opinion then and what transpired to the point that now you are at the farthest end of the diagram in Figure 14-1? Explain.

4. How important is credibility? Identify five people who have at least one component of credibility. Name the person and the component. List five people who, in your opinion, do not have credibility. Name the person and the component he or she lacks.

Online Activities

1. Select a persuasive speech topic on which you have a firm solid anchor position. Now, structure a coherent persuasive message directly opposed to your stance. Research and cite five competent and credible online sources supporting this view. Outline your speech according to the motivated sequence format in Chapter 14. Insert the supporting material where appropriate. Be ethical. Could you put together a reasonable realistic and achievable call for action? Does this alter your approach if you now had to present your original anchor position?

2. Assume this premise: The board of directors of a major television network is about to make a secret deal to sell the network to a business group of people disliked by the public. The evening newscaster discovers the deal and reveals the plans on the air. The deal falls apart. The network president, who stands to personally profit by millions of dollars, brings the newsman in for a persuasive speech to convince him to change his position. With that setup in mind, get the list of Unethical Communication Behaviors from Chapter 14 and go to YouTube and view "Network (1976)—Ned Beatty—The world is a business." How many of the unethical communication behaviors were committed in this speech?

3. List the five stages of the motivated sequence. Follow along as you go to YouTube and view Gordon Gekko's "Greed is Good" Full Speech. Cite each stage of the motivated sequence and how Gekko met that component. Whether you agree or disagree with the premise, that is a well-structured persuasive speech!

Name: _____

Date: _____

Chapter 14: Worksheet #1

1. Define persuasion.

2. Identify five unethical communication behaviors.

3. What are the two desired outcomes of a persuasive speech?

4. We can categorize persuasion by approach. What are the two choices?

5. When is indirect persuasion ethical and justified?

(To download this worksheet as a Word document, visit the companion website at www.oup.com/us/adler.)

Name: _____

Date: _____

Chapter 14: Worksheet #2

1. What are the stages of the motivated sequence?

2. Identify six logical fallacies to avoid in a persuasive speech.

3. Define credibility.

4. What are the three "C's" of credibility? Define each one.

(To download this worksheet as a Word document, visit the companion website at www.oup.com/us/adler.)

Appendix A: Chapter Outlines

Chapter 1: Outline

I.   Communication defined: the process of creating meaning through symbolic interaction

A: A linear model of people interacting uses channels (including mediated communication) to convey messages from different fields of experiences (environments). This is similar to exchanging injections of communication back and forth.

B: A transactional model shows both sending and receiving is simultaneous. At any given moment we are capable of receiving, decoding, and responding and overcoming noise at the same time the other communicator is receiving, decoding, and responding while overcoming noise.

II.   Characteristics of communication: It is a symbolic relational process, not individual (not something we do to others but rather something we do with others). We use things, processes, ideas, and events arbitrarily with agreed-upon linguistic rules and customs to make communication possible.

III.   Types of communication include intrapersonal, dyadic/interpersonal, small group, organizational, public, and mass.

IV.   Communication challenges abound in this changing world. Technology has replaced face-to-face speech as the primary form of communication for today's college student.

A.   Social media differs from mass communication in the variable size of the target audience. While mediated communication and face-to-face share many similarities there are differences in richness, synchronous communication, and permanence. Social media is used for information, relationships, personal identity, and entertainment.

B.   To communicate competently with social media you must choose the best medium, be careful what you post, be considerate, balance with face time, and be safe.

V.   Communication is used to satisfy physical, identity, social, and practical needs.

VI.   Effective communicators have communication competence.

A.   Communication competence is defined as achieving one's goals in a manner that, ideally, maintains or enhances the relationship in which it occurs.

B.   There is no one "ideal" way to communicate because competence is situational and relational at the same time.

C.   Competence can be learned providing the student is open to a wide range of behaviors, has the ability to choose the most appropriate behavior, develops skill at performing these behaviors, and employs empathy and perspective taking with the cognitive complexity to construct a variety of frameworks for viewing an issue. Self-monitoring and commitment to the relationship are also necessary for effective communication competence.

VII.   Recognizing what communication is "not" helps avoid misconceptions.

A.   Communication does not always require complete understanding nor will it solve all problems.

B.   Communication is not simple and more is not always better.

C.   Very often the "meaning" of the communication rests in people, not in words.

Chapter 2: Outline

I.   Nothing is more fundamental to understanding how we communicate than our sense of self.

A.   Self-concept is the relatively stable perceptions that each of us holds about ourselves. This mental mirror reflects our view of our "self."

B.   Personality is the characteristic ways you think and behave across a variety of situations. The reflected appraisal describes how you develop an image of your "self" from the way you think others view you. We particularly value the opinion of our significant others as vital to our self-esteem.

II.   Our self-concept affects our behavior, which in turn affects how others view us, and we read that reaction and apply it to our self-concept.

A.   The self-fulfilling prophecy occurs when a person expects an outcome and behaves in a way to make the outcome more likely to occur.

B.   The self-fulfilling prophecy is an important force in communication as we often behave how we are perceived we are going to behave, thus reinforcing the perception.

III.   Just like others' perception of us often influences our interaction, our perception of others affects our interaction with them.

A.   We use a selection process to collect data for our perception. We pay attention to contrasts and change, we have motives, and we are influenced by moods.

B.   We arrange the information we gather in an organization, classifying people according to physical constructs, role constructs, interaction constructs, and psychological constructs.

C.   Our interpretation offers some sense of our perceptions. The degree of involvement, relational satisfaction, personal experience, assumptions, expectations, and knowledge all influence interpretation.

D.   The negotiation of this collected data is influenced by physiological things such as age, health and nutrition, biological factors, and neurology.

E.   Cultural influences provide a filter for interpretation. Sex and gender roles also affect perception; so do occupational and relational roles.

F.   We all have our own story, our narrative, a framework of explaining behavior and shaping communication.

IV.   Shared narratives may be desirable but are hard to achieve. Often we undertake the process of attaching meaning to behavior. This attribution leads to some common perceptual tendencies.

A.   We make snap judgments based on stereotyping. We judge ourselves more charitably than we judge others, we pay more attention to negative impressions than positive ones, and we are influenced by what is most obvious.

B.   We also err when we cling to first impressions even if later proved wrong, and we tend to assume others similar to us are "like" us.

V.   One solution to overcoming these tendencies is to have the ability to apply empathy.

A.   Perspective taking gives us the ability to take on the other's viewpoint. While not to be confused with sympathy, empathy identifies with the other. Empathy allows for understanding without requiring you to agree with the reasons.

B.   Good intentions and empathy are best used to handle perception checking. This involves describing the behavior, offering at least two interpretations, and making a request for clarification.

VI.   The communication strategies people use to influence how others view them are called identity management.

A.   Our perceived self is a reflection of self-concept—who, in moments of honest reflection, we believe we are. Our presenting self is the way we want to appear to others.

B.   The term face is used to describe the presenting self and facework is the verbal and nonverbal ways we maintain our presenting image.

C.   We have multiple identities we present in a multiple of settings. We perform in tandem with others, we collaborate, as we sometimes think we are expected to perform.

D.   We do this both consciously and unconsciously; sometimes we are aware of the image we are projecting but at other times we slip into roles without planning or consciously trying. We differ in the degree of identity management depending on our self-monitoring.

VII.   We usually manage our identities to follow social rules.

A.   Social rules govern our behaviors as we strive to meet expectations and to accomplish personal goals.

B.   While mediated communication limits potential for accurate perception, it is used for identity management. Strangers change their age, history, personality, and even gender. This form of deception, known as "cat-fishing," gained national prominence recently with the exposé of a fraud perpetuated on a nationally known collegiate football figure.

C.   There is a fine line of distinction between managing identities and remaining honest. The decision must come from within as complete self-disclosure, absolute blunt honesty, is rarely appropriate.

Chapter 3: Outline

I.   Defining culture is not easy. The simplest definition is to say it is the language, values, beliefs, traditions, and customs people share and learn.

A.   Coculture is a group within the culture. Membership in a coculture often shapes the nature of communication.

B.   Salience describes the weight we attach to cultural characteristics.

II.   Cultural differences are generalizations but cultural values and norms shape communication.

A.   Cultures valuing the individual more are said to be individualistic, whereas collectivistic cultures put group above self. Two distinct ways members of various cultures deliver messages are high context and low context.

B.   Cultures have ways of coping with unpredictable situations. The level of uncertainty avoidance reflects reaction to ambiguous circumstances. The extent of the gap between social groups who possess resources and those who don't is called power distance. Greater or lesser power distance signals class separation or class equality.

C.   Some cultures value silence in communication whereas others insert talking as required social acceptance. There is a tendency to regard some cultures as masculine, feminine, and androgynous.

D.   Race and ethnicity mostly involve superficial qualities but have social significance. Stereotyping and prejudice often accompany noted differences between ethnicities and race. Regional differences shape feelings of belonging and are often indicated via accents.

E.   Cultures attach communicative value in gender identity and sexual orientation, religion, physical ability or disability, age, and socioeconomic status.

III.   Different verbal and nonverbal communication codes hamper cross-cultural communication.

A.   Language and identity are closely tied to prestige.

B.   Verbal codes such as directness or indirectness, elaborate or succinct, and formality or informality affect characterizations and perceptions.

C.   Nonverbal codes offer a range of interpretations and symbolism. Proximity, eye contact, touch, volume, and gestures are all measured with an eye toward culture.

IV.   Decoding the verbal and nonverbal systems across cultures is a challenge.

A.   Translation does not guarantee clarity.

B.   Comprehending patterns of thought is more important than literal translation.

V.   The best development of intercultural communication competence hinges on a wide range of appropriate behaviors.

A.   Increased contact produces contact hypothesis and better relationships.

B.   A tolerance for ambiguity averts fear and apprehension of the "different."

C.   Open-mindedness can combat ethnocentrism: the attitude that one's culture is superior to another.

D.   Education, knowledge, and skill are developed through passive observation, active strategies, and self-disclosure.

E.   Most of all, patience and perseverance reward effort. Culture shock or adjustment shock causes confusion, disorientation, resentment, and disappointment. Have patience. Continue the effort.

Chapter 4: Outline

I.   Language is defined as a collection of symbols governed by rules and used to convey messages between individuals.

A.   Language is symbolic, with the meanings resting in people, not the words.

B.   Language is rule governed. Phonological rules govern sound, syntactic rules govern structure, semantic rules deal with meaning, and pragmatic rules cover interactions.

C.   The use of language shapes attitudes through naming, credibility, status, sexism, and racism.

D.   How we use language reflects back on us through power, affiliation, attraction and interest, and responsibility.

II.   Most language misunderstandings are easily remedied if you recognize them.

A.   Words or phrases having more than one meaning are called equivocal language. Often misinterpreted because they can be taken "the wrong way," equivocal phrasing can also be ambiguous and misleading.

B.   Relative words gain their meaning by comparison; the misunderstanding arises from variations in contrast.

C.   Slang is a language used by a group of people whose members belong to a similar coculture, whereas jargon is a specialized vocabulary that functions as a kind of shorthand for people with common knowledge or experience.

D.   Overly abstract language uses objects, events, and ideas to describe varying degrees of specificity. A book is not just a book: it can be hardback or paperback, a textbook or a novel, large print or on an e-reader.

E.   Abstract language refers to events or objects only vaguely. It is used to avoid confrontations, to hint, or to generalize, thus causing confusion and misunderstanding.

III.   Three bad linguistic habits often result in disruptive language that stimulates trouble.

A.   Confusing facts and opinions: an opinion statement masked as a factual statement leads to conflict.

B.   Confusing facts and inferences: arriving at a conclusion from interpretation and not labeling the inferential statement as opinion leads to difficulty.

C.   Using emotive language that sounds descriptive but signals attitude causes problems.

IV.   Evasive language is designed to mislead or antagonize. It purposefully avoids clear communication.

A.   To substitute a pleasant term for a more direct but potentially less pleasant one is to use euphemisms.

B.   To be deliberately vague in a way that can be interpreted in more than one way is to use equivocation.

V.   There are similarities and there are differences in how the genders use language.

A.   In terms of content, men are more likely to talk about recreation, technology, and nightlife, whereas women tend to favor discussing relationships, friends, family, and emotions.

B.   Women concentrate more on personal problems first; men joke and kid around and tease.

C.   Men use language more to accomplish a task, women to support, demonstrate, and share values.

D.   Women ask questions; men make statements.

E.   Similarities exist and the differences blur when men and women use profanity and vocal fillers, have shared occupations, and exist in mutually similar socioeconomic strata.

F.   Often psychological sex roles play more of a influence than biological sex in how the genders use language.

Chapter 5: Outline

I.   Listening and hearing are not the same thing.

A.   Listening occurs when the brain reconstructs electrochemical impulses into a representation of the original sound and gives them meaning.

B.   Listening requires attending, understanding, responding, and remembering.

C.   Listening fidelity is the degree of congruence between what a listener understands and what the sender was attempting to communicate.

D.   Listening is not a natural process where all listeners receive the same message.

E.   Mindful listening requires effort whereas mindless listening is passive with low-level processing of information.

II.   There are several faulty listening behaviors we all possess.

A.   Pseudolistening is to imitate the real thing; selective listening responds only to a part of the message.

B.   Defensive listening turns innocent remarks into attacks and ambushing collects information in order to attack back.

C.   Insulated listeners avoid and insensitive listeners are unable to look beyond the words and take things at face value.

D.   Stage hogging takes place when listeners turn all conversations onto themselves.

III.   The causes of poor listening are many.

A.   Message overload, rapid thought, and psychological and physical noise are some reasons for poor listening.

B.   Other reasons are hearing problems, faulty assumptions, talking has more advantages, cultural differences, and media influences.

IV.   There are a number of reasons people invest effort into listening.

A.   Task-oriented listening aims to be informational listening by looking for key ideas, asking questions, paraphrasing, and taking notes.

B.   Relational listening aims at emotional connections by taking the time to listen for unexpressed thoughts and feelings and encouraging further comments.

C.   Analytical listening aims to enhance the relationship and understand the message. This is done by listening before evaluating, separating the message from the speaker, and searching for value.

D.   Applying analytical listening to see if a message stands up to scrutiny is one element of critical listening. The goal here is to examine the speaker's evidence and reasoning, gauge the speaker's credibility, and examine the emotional appeals being employed.

V.   Supportive listening is aimed to help the speaker deal with personal dilemmas.

A.   Using mediated communication for counseling and advice has grown into an industry of its own for medical conditions, eating disorders, sexual orientation, divorce, shyness, addiction, loneliness, safety, and exercise because of, along with other factors, the online anonymity support avenues that prompt faster revelations in a shorter period of time.

B.   Generally speaking, women are more likely than men to give supportive responses when presented with another person's problems.

C.   Supportive responses come in the form of advising, judging, analyzing, questioning, comforting, prompting, and reflecting.

D.   Before committing, be sure your support is welcomed. You should evaluate the situation, the other person, and your own strengths and weaknesses.

Chapter 6: Outline

I.   Messages expressed through nonlinguistic means are nonverbal communication.

A.   Such messages do have communicative value, although they are primarily relational.

B.   While nonverbal communication is ambiguous, it differs from verbal communication because of complexity and flow.

C.   Nonverbal encoding and decoding skills are strong predictors of popularity, attractiveness, and socioemotional well-being.

II.   There are important differences in the way people use and understand nonverbal behavior.

A.   Cultures have varying nonverbal languages in gestures, the use of silence, the use of space and distance, eye contact, and even frequency of interruptions.

B.   Gender roles are often stereotypical, but generally speaking women tend to smile more, use more facial expressions, touch others more, stand closer to others, and make more eye contact.

III.   Nonverbal communication functions along with verbal communication for more effective communication.

A.   Nonverbal communication uses repeating to aid in memory, substituting to communicate emblems with precise meaning within a cultural group, and complementing to reinforce or go along with verbal communication.

B.   The process of placing emphasis on oral messages is the nonverbal function of accenting. Nonverbal communication is also used for regulating—signaling the beginning or the end of communication and controlling the pace.

C.   Two other nonverbal communication functions are the often-misunderstood practice of contradicting and the usually uncomfortable art of deceiving.

IV.   There are many tools at our disposal for sending nonverbal messages.

A.   Body movements are the most noticeable and include posture and gestures.

B.   The face and the eyes have powerful nonverbal impact. Expressions reflecting many emotions are called affect blends, where two or more expressions show different emotions.

C.   One great nonverbal tool is the voice. Paralanguage is the word used to describe nonverbal but vocal messages such as volume, emphasis, tone, speed, pitch, pauses, and any disfluency such as stammering and vocal fillers.

D.   Appearance is a message sender involving physical attractiveness, clothing, and hygiene.

E.   Physical touch can "speak" volumes. The use of distance and the way people and animals use space is called proxemics. Intimate distance is from skin contact to about 18 inches out from the body. Personal distance starts at about 18 inches and can go out four feet. Social distance starts at four feet and extends to twelve feet. Public distance goes from twelve feet on out. Distance is something we like to decide depending on how we feel toward the other person, the context of the conversation, and our personal goals.

F.   Where personal space is our invisible bubble we carry around and adjust depending on the influences, territoriality is fixed. A room, a building, a neighborhood, or even a larger area to which we assume some kind of "rights" is our territory. "My desk," "my office," "my yard," and "my city" are typical expressions of territoriality. We grant people with higher status more personal territory and greater privacy.

G.   The physical environment people create reflects and shapes nonverbal interactions, and the study of how human beings use and structure time (known as chronemics) expresses both intentional and unintentional messages.

V.   Knowledge about nonverbal messages can improve communication skills, can allow the listener to be more attuned to others, and can make communicators more aware of the messages they send.

A.   It pays to tune out words and focus on meaning, usually sent nonverbally.

B.   Since nonverbal communication is ambiguous, always perform perception-checking practices.

C.   Pay attention to your own nonverbal practices. Record a video of "you being you" in an average conversation and then turn off the volume. What are you "saying" by what you are "doing"? That is the message others get.

Chapter 7: Outline

I.   Factors influencing our choice of relational partners include superficial as well as contemplative reasons.

A.   Appearance, similarity, complementary characteristics, and reciprocal attraction affect our relationship choices.

B.   We favor individuals we deem capable of competence and use self-disclosure to build liking.

C.   In many cases relationships form due to proximity and the social exchange theory of costs versus rewards.

II.   All dyadic communication is contextually interpersonal communication.

A.   Qualitatively interpersonal communication occurs when people treat one another as unique individuals.

B.   Impersonal communication is the opposite, peripheral and fleetingly superficial.

C.   While mediated communication reduces the frequency and quality of face-to-face interaction, it is used by some to enhance the quantity and quality of interpersonal communication. The social support and asynchronous nature of mediated communication contribute to an easy, anonymous courage, resulting in greater self-disclosure.

III.   Virtually every verbal statement contains two kinds of messages.

A.   Content messages focus on the subject being discussed.

B.   Relational messages express feelings and attitudes.

C.   The dimensions of relational communications include affinity, respect, immediacy, and control.

D.   Metacommunication is a term used to describe messages that refer to other messages.

IV.   A developmental model of the rise and fall of relationships contains phrases of coming together and coming apart.

A.   Coming together is indicated by initiating, experimenting, intensifying, integrating, and bonding.

B.   Differentiating starts the process of coming apart, followed by circumscribing, stagnating, avoiding, and terminating.

C.   Not all relationships follow all the progressive steps, and they usually are fluid and transitory between the stages.

V.   Seeking important but often incompatible goals in a relationship results in a dialectical model that demonstrates the creation of dialectical tensions.

A.   These tensions include a connection–autonomy dialectic, a predictability–novelty dialectic, and an openness–privacy dialectic that requires agile juggling.

B.   Managing these dialectical tensions requires the strategy of recognizing denial, overcoming disorientation, using a selection process for the alteration between one end or the other, compartmentalizing different areas in a segmentation tactic, using moderation or compromise to handle the tension, and reframing that could result in reaffirmation.

VI.   Even the closest relationships involve a mixture of alternating "we" with "me."

A.   Intimacy is defined as a close union, contact, association, or acquaintance.

B.   Physical closeness, intellectual sharing, emotion involving an exchange of important feeling, and shared activities provide various states of intimacy.

C.   Women appear more willing to share their thoughts and feelings, and cherish personal talk. Men grow close to one another by doing things together. Generally speaking, men value doing for or with as intimacy.

D.   Personal preferences influence intimacy styles more than gender. People typically orient to either words of affirmation, quality time, acts of service, gifts, or physical touch.

E.   Cultural variances affect how much intimacy is desired.

VII.   The process of deliberately revealing information about oneself that is significant and that would not normally be known is called self-disclosure.

A.   The social penetration model has as its first dimension the breadth of information volunteered. This includes the range of subjects discussed. The second dimension is the depth of shifting from non-revealing to personal messages.

B.   Another model of self-disclosure is reflected in the Johari Window, where your likes and dislikes, goals, secrets, and needs are then divided into a part you know about and the part you don't know about imposed one atop the other with things others know about you and things you want to keep to yourself. There is an open area and a blind area, a hidden area and an unknown area, and items move from one area to the other through self-disclosure.

C. Self-disclosure is influenced by culture and usually occurs in dyads. It is usually symmetrical and occurs incrementally. While relatively scarce, self-disclosure uses the guidelines of: is the person important to you, is the risk reasonable, is it appropriate, will it be reciprocated, and is it constructive, clear, and understandable?

VIII. Three common alternatives to self-disclosure are lies, equivocation, and hinting.

A. Altruistic lies are defined as intended to be harmless or even helpful. Yet the discovery of lies causes feelings of dismay and betrayal.

B. Equivocation has perceived value as a balance between harsh truths and lying.

C. Hints are more direct than equivocal language but depend on the other person's ability to pick up the unexpressed message.

Chapter 8: Outline

I.   Personal relationships are a lot like the weather. The communication climate of a relationship refers to the emotional tone involved. The degree to which people see themselves as valued affects the climate.

A.   Confirming responses offer recognition, acknowledgment, and endorsement.

B.   Disconfirming responses show disagreement, disrespect, disinterest, and negativity.

C.   Escalatory spirals build from one disconfirming message affecting the climate to a stronger one to an even stronger one to a full-fledged storm! Avoidance spirals lessen communication through withdrawal, disregard, less investment, and even ignoring the other person involved.

D.   Positive communication climates come about with the Gibb categories of evaluation versus description, control versus problem orientation, strategy versus spontaneity, neutrality versus empathy, superiority versus equality, and certainty versus provisionalism.

II.   Communication conflict is the expressed struggle between at least two interdependent parties who perceive incompatible goals, scarce rewards, and interference from the other parties in achieving their goals.

A.   Conflict is expressed through nonassertion, direct aggression, passive aggression, indirect communication, and assertion.

B.   Assertive communication messages are by far the most productive and involve using behavioral descriptions, interpretation of the other's behavior, a description of personal feelings, a description of consequences, and a statement of intention.

C.   Men and women approach conflict differently, with men thriving on competition and women gravitating toward emotional connections.

D.   Cultural variances offer differences in dealing with conflict such as individualistic goals versus collectivist concerns.

III.   Every conflict is a struggle, to which there are four possible outcomes: Win-Lose, Lose-Lose, Compromise, or Win-Win.

A.   Win-Win satisfies the needs of everyone involved. The steps to achieving Win-Win are: identify your problem and unmet needs, make a date, describe your problem and needs, partner check back, solicit partner's needs, check understanding of partner's needs, and negotiate a solution.

B.   Steps to negotiation are: identify and define the conflict, generate a number of possible solutions, evaluate the alternative solutions, decide on the best solution, and follow up.

Chapter 9: Outline

I.   A group consists of a small collection of people who interact with each other, over time, in order to reach goals.

A.   A team is a group but members work together on a higher level. Teams share clear and inspiring goals, a results-driven structure, competent team members, unified commitment, a collaborative climate, standards of excellence, external support and recognition, and principled leadership.

B.   Virtual groups are teams who interact with one another through mediated communication, without meeting face to face. This form of interaction has advantages in terms of ease and expediency of overcoming geographical challenges and leveling the status differences of rank, age, and gender.

II.   Two forces drive group communication: (1) group goals, which are the outcomes you seek to accomplish together, and (2) individual goals, the personal motives of each member.

A.   Most groups meet to achieve a collective task, but social goals of fraternization are equally important.

B.   Individuals participate in groups for many personal reasons; these can become disruptive if the goal consists of a hidden agenda, because it is often in conflict with the group goals.

III.   All groups and teams have rules and all groups have norms.

A.   A rule is the official guideline.

B.   Norms are the unspoken standards. Social norms govern how members relate and procedural norms are for operations. Task norms govern how members get the job done.

IV.   The more complex the structure of groups, the greater effect this has on the flow of information.

A.   All-channel networks allow group members to share the same information. In a chain network information moves sequentially. In a wheel network, clearinghouse gatekeepers are used to disperse information.

B.   Patterns of behavior by members within the group or team are called roles. Formal roles are assigned and designated. Informal roles serve functions but are rarely acknowledged by the group in words. Informal roles fall into two categories: task help and social roles, Other roles are used for maintenance, to continue the relationships and dysfunctional roles, which are unfortunately too common in groups or teams, prevent the group from being effective.

C.	Three role-related problems occur when (1) important informal roles go unfilled, (2) competition causes divisiveness, or (3) one member becomes a victim of role fixation (acting out a role whether or not the situation requires it).

V.	All groups or teams have a leader or leaders.

A.	The authoritarian leadership style relies on legitimate, coercive, and reward power to influence others. In the democratic leadership style members share in the decision making. In the laissez-faire leadership style the leader relinquishes the power and leaves the group rudderless. A situational leadership style changes with the circumstances.

B.	Transactional operators are motivated primarily by personal glory. Team players work to keep members happy and to maintain harmony. Transformational leaders respect the power of teamwork and encourage positive morale.

C.	Even in groups that begin with no official leaders, a member or members will become the emergent leader.

VI.	If every group or team has a leader then there must be followers.

A.	Isolates are indifferent and communicate little outside their environment. Bystanders tend to hang back and watch. Participants attempt to have an impact. Activists are more engaged and passionate. Diehards will, literally, sacrifice themselves for the cause.

B.	Followers hold the power. This ability to influence others has many guises. Legitimate power arises from the title or position one holds. Expert power comes from knowledge and competence. Connection power exists when a member has the ability to develop relationships that help the group. Reward power is gained by granting or promising a pay-off. Coercive power involves threats, intimidation, and punishment.

C.	Referent power comes from the respect, liking, and trust of others.

D.	Power is group centered. A leader only has the power granted by the group. Power is distributed among group members and occurs in degrees; it is not an either-or concept.

Chapter 10: Outline

I.   In most cases groups can produce more solutions to a problem than individuals.

A.   Problem-solving groups are more effective because they have more resources, an improved rate of accuracy, more commitment, and increased diversity.

B.   Groups are justified if the job is beyond the capacity of one person, if individual tasks are interdependent, if there is more than one possible decision or solution, and if there is potential for disagreement.

II.   Groups are most effective when members feel good about one another.

A.   Cohesiveness, the degree to which members feel connected with and committed to the group, helps a group to be effective.

B.   Cohesiveness is boosted when there are shared or compatible goals, progress toward those goals, and shared norms and values.

C.   Other contributors to cohesiveness are the lack of perceived threat between members, interdependence of members, and a perceived threat outside the group.

D.   Two other components of cohesiveness are the feelings of mutual attraction and friendship and shared group experiences.

III.   Many problem-solving groups develop along predictable stages when organizing and strategizing.

A.   Members approach the initial orientation stage quite tentatively. Once the reason for the group is identified there is a conflict stage of positions and viewpoints. Give-and-take discussions should progress to a sense of unity and cooperation; thus, the emergence stage develops as the members become a group. Once the group works together the members support and defend each other in the reinforcement stage.

B.   Problem-solving groups use a number of formats and approaches to present their results. Breakout groups are offshoots of a larger group, problem census approaches might be used to make a list of ideas to discuss. A focus group does not decide the outcome but rather provides solicited feedback.

C.   Parliamentary procedure provides specific rules for discussion and decision making. A panel discussion involves roundtable contributions with audience members observing and eavesdropping. A symposium presentation occurs when the members divide the topic and each delivers information uninterrupted. Forum groups encourage input and participation from nonmembers. Dialogue encourages give-and-take and listening to others without superiority with a goal toward understanding.

IV.   Often emotions hamper rational differences of opinion in a group, so a template for reflective thinking and decision making is useful.

A.   A structured approach for a problem-solving group would be to identify the problem, analyze the problem, develop creative solutions, evaluate possible solutions, implement the plan, and follow up on the solution.

B.   The decision-making process has several options. Majority control allows quick votes but could exclude 49% of the members. Expert opinion works well if someone has the knowledge but stumbles if not everyone accepts the expert. Minority control has a few decide for the many but overlooks the input of the many. Authority rule is autocratic, efficient, and, at times, dictatorial, but failure to consult members can leave them feeling ordered rather than asked. Consensus means all members agree on the decision. The problem there is that full and complete agreement is very difficult to achieve without compromise.

V.   Even groups with the best intentions encounter stumbling blocks to effectiveness.

A.   Information underload, the scarcity of accurate and current input, hinders good results. Information overload can overwhelm group members by causing complications and distractions. Unequal participation is the bane of all experienced group members. Unfair balance of responsibilities, a reluctant or absent member, a dysfunctional member demonstrating lack of cooperation: these bog down progress and stifle results.

B.   A strong tendency to "go along to get along," the pressure to conform, often overwhelms dissent when a contrary perspective could be useful.

Chapter 11: Outline

I.   The three steps to preparing a speech are: choose a topic, determine your purpose, and find information.

A.   Pick a topic that interests you. Pick a topic early. More time means more research and practice.

B.   The purpose statement of your speech is expressed in a complete sentence that describes exactly what you want your speech to accomplish. This specific purpose should stem from your overall general purpose to inform, persuade, or entertain.

C.   The purpose statement should be results-oriented, specific, and realistic.

D.   The thesis statement tells your listeners the general idea.

II.   Two things to always consider in preparing a speech: the audience and the occasion.

A.   Audience analysis involves identifying and adapting your remarks to your listeners.

B.   Audience members are there for a reason. You need to know the audience purpose. Characteristics such as age, gender, cultural diversity, group membership, and so on are audience demographics. What is the audience attitude? What are their beliefs and values?

C.   A second step in preparation takes into account the time, place, and audience expectations.

III.   Now you are ready to find information.

A.   Use online research if you can verify its credibility, objectivity, and currency. Is the material accurate and truthful, is it non-biased, and is it recent?

B.   Use library catalog sources, reference works, periodicals, databases, and interviews for accurate information. Survey research is another venue to explore for source material and involves distributing questionnaires to peers and other contributors.

IV.   You are getting the material ready, so how about the fear of giving a speech?

A.   Facilitative communication apprehension involves some nervousness and anxiety. That is to be expected. Confidence reinforced by practice and more practice addresses the usual butterflies common to all.

B.   Debilitative communication apprehension involves panic, the fight-or-flight reflex, and crippling self-doubt. Previous negative experiences, irrational thinking, the fallacy of catastrophic failure (anticipating that something awful will happen), the fallacy of perfection expected from the listeners, the fallacy of approval (where you think you have to please everyone), and the fallacy of overgeneralization (where you blow things totally out of proportion) all contribute to debilitative anxiety.

C.   Fight back by using the nervousness to your advantage, understanding the difference between rational concerns and irrational fears, maintaining a receiver orientation (this is for them and not about you), keeping a positive attitude where your visualization is one of success, and being prepared. Practice ahead of time and anticipate all possible challenges.

V.   The decision on how to present the speech is your next step of preparation.

A.   An extemporaneous speech is planned in advance and presented in a conversational tone. An impromptu speech is spontaneous and unplanned. A manuscript speech is written out and then read word for word. A memorized speech is learned and presented without notes.

B.   Other delivery considerations include appearance, movement, posture, facial expressions, gestures, and eye contact.

C.   Auditory aspects of delivery include volume, rate, pitch, word choice, and articulation.

D.   The four most common articulation challenges are deletion, substitution, addition, and slurring.

Chapter 12: Outline

I.   Building a speech starts with a strong foundation. The outline is that foundation.

A.   A working outline is a construction tool to map out your speech. This is for your eyes only, informal and rough, used to refine and solidify ideas.

B.   A formal outline uses a consistent format and set of symbols.

C.   Speaking notes are used to jog your memory. These are usually brief phrases and keywords organized to aid the flow and progression of the speech.

D.   Following a standard format contributes to neatness, ease of scanning, and coordination of main points and sub-points.

II.   The outline must be organized in a logical pattern.

A.   Time patterns organize things in chronological order: first came this, then this, then lastly this.

B.   Space patterns are organized according to area: moving from east to west or smaller to larger.

C.   Topic patterns follow types or categories: well-known to less familiar, classifications that progress to the next step or stage.

D.   Problem-solution patterns describe what is wrong and propose a way to make things better. This is a popular format for persuasive speeches.

E.   Cause-effect patterns discuss what happened and then the consequences of what happened.

F.   Monroe's motivated sequence gets attention, addresses a need, offers satisfaction, paints a beneficial visualization, and then calls for action.

III.   Moving from one portion or component of the speech to the next is accomplished by using transitions.

A.   Transitions help relate one point to the next. They move the flow from highlight to highlight and soothe the hectic stop-start of presenting.

B.   Transitions connect and bond the components of the outline pattern to conversational delivery.

IV.   Every speech starts with an introduction.

A.   The first goal of an introduction is to capture the attention of the audience. There are many approaches possible, but the most important thing to remember is you want the audience to pay attention.

B.   An effective introduction states the speaker's thesis by previewing main points.

C.   The beginning of your speech sets the mood and tone of the speech. You must demonstrate the importance of your topic to the audience and establish your credibility.

V.   Although some anxious speakers have their doubts, every speech has a conclusion. It will end!

A.   The conclusion should restate the thesis, review main points, and provide a memorable final remark.

B.   Bad conclusions ruin an otherwise good speech, so remember the four "don'ts": don't end abruptly, don't ramble, don't introduce new points, and don't apologize.

VI.   Charisma and character do not guarantee the audience's attention unless you have supporting material.

A.   The role of supporting material is to clarify, prove, make interesting, and make memorable.

B.   Various types of supporting material include definition, example, statistic, analogy/comparison-contrast, anecdote, and quotation/testimony.

C.   The narration style of presenting means telling a story or relating an incident. Citation uses someone else's work; you are using it as a statement of fact.

Chapter 13: Outline

I.   There is a lot of information out there, almost too much. How do you cope?

A.   Information overload is a form of stress where people get confused and have trouble sorting out the wheat from the chaff.

B.   Information anxiety results in mind clutter and frustration over what to discard and what to turn into knowledge.

C.   Effective public speakers use information to give knowledge to the listeners.

II.   Informative speeches primarily have to do with content and purpose.

A.   Content speeches deal with objects, processes, events, and concepts.

B.   Speeches dealing with purpose involve descriptions, explanations, and instructions.

C.   Informative speeches tend to be noncontroversial and do not attempt to change the audience's opinions.

D.   Persuasive speeches advocate change and expect resistance to acceptance.

III.   The techniques of informative speaking help an audience understand and care.

A.   Formulate a specific informative purpose statement. Create information hunger. Make it easy to listen. Use clear, simple language. Use a clear organization and structure.

B.   It is very beneficial to use supportive material effectively. Emphasize important points. Generate audience involvement and encourage audience participation. Use signposts that emphasize upcoming material. Use visual aids.

C.   There are a wide variety of choices for visual aids, such as objects and models, diagrams, word charts, number charts, pie charts, bar charts, column charts, line charts, chalk and whiteboards, posters and pads, handouts, projectors, power point, Prezi, keynote, video, vocal citations, audio, and physical demonstrations.

D.   Visual aids should be evaluated for simplicity, size, attractiveness, appropriateness, and reliability.

Chapter 14: Outline

I.   Persuasion is the process of motivating someone, through communication, to change a particular belief, attitude, or behavior.

A.   Persuasion is not coercive but it is usually incremental.

B.   The social judgment theory is used by listeners to compare the opinions of the speaker to ones they already hold.

C.   The preexisting opinion is known as the anchor and any movement or change goes along a diagram of latitude of acceptance, latitude of rejection, and latitude of noncommitment.

D.   Persuasion is interactive. Persuasion differs from coercion in that it is ethical. Ethical persuasion is communication in the best interest of the audience that does not depend on false or misleading information to change the audience's attitude or behavior.

II.   There are several types of persuasion depending on the proposition being advanced.

A.   Propositions of fact come up when there are two or more sides and the audience is being asked to choose.

B.   Propositions of value explore the worth of an idea, person, or object.

C.   Propositions of policy recommend a specific course of action.

III.   Persuasion offers two possible desired outcomes. Convincing the audience to change a way of thinking is one desired outcome. The other is to set about to actuate an audience into a specific behavior.

A.   Direct persuasion is used to make the message clear early in the speech.

B.   Indirect persuasion deemphasizes the purpose to allow a hostile or unfriendly audience time to adjust to the proposal.

IV.   Persuasion has been called a "reason-giving discourse." The technique, therefore, of creating a persuasive message involves proposing claims and backing those claims up with accurate reasons.

A.   There must be a clear, persuasive purpose with a message that is structured carefully.

B.   The speaker needs to describe the problem, describe the solution, describe the desired audience response, and then combine the solution with the desired audience response. One recommended way to do this is to use the motivated sequence.

C.   Solid evidence is mandatory in persuasion, and this includes emotional evidence that evokes feelings.

V.   Too often the ethical approach of persuasion is hampered by errors in logic. A fallacy of logic can negate any possible movement the listener might have been contemplating.

A.   The ad hominem fallacy attacks the person instead of the argument. A reductio ad absurdum fallacy takes the argument to ridiculous extremes. Either-or fallacy proposals issue ultimatums and set up false alternatives.

B.   Additional logical errors take place when the speaker uses the _post hoc fallacy. This mistakenly assumes one event caused another because they happened sequentially. An argumentum ad verecundiam involves relying on the testimony of someone who has a title or fame but is not an expert. Mass appeal is often used via the argumentum ad populum, also called bandwagon. Just because many approve does not mean it is the correct decision.

VI.   High on the list of priorities for a persuasive speech is the need to appreciate your target audience.

A.   Persuasive speakers should establish a common ground and organize according to the expected response.

B.   The speaker needs to neutralize potential hostility and build credibility as a speaker. To have credibility means you are believable.

C.   Competence means expertise on the subject. Character implies trustworthiness, and charisma means likability.

D.   Aristotle referred to these qualities as ethos to mean credibility, pathos to appeal to emotion, and logos to affect reasoning and logic.

Appendix B: Review Questions

Chapter 1: Answers to Review Questions

Your answers should include the following points:

1. Re-examine the Scenarios laid out in the Self-Assessment exercise and determine the qualities, advantages, and benefits of each option. There are situations where text and Twitter is inappropriate, places where restraint and self-editing is justified, and a circumstance where privacy boundaries must be respected. There is one scenario where future income hinges on the correct decision. Reread the text and make your selections based on the guidance and content of the material.

2. The definition of human communication and the characteristics it embodies establishes the foundation of this textbook. Review Chapter 1 extensively.

3. Not all mediated communication is intended for mass audiences. The similarity with face-to-face is equivalent to whispering, using your indoor voice, or shouting at a football game. The sender decides the message and the receiver. Review the components dealing with mediated versus face-to-face communication and the section titled "Understanding Social Media."

    The differences occur in three ways. Have you experienced this in personal situations?

4. Each type is used by communicators on a daily basis. You should be prepared to give examples. See the section of this chapter titled "Types of Communication."

5. Review the component in this chapter titled "Functions of Communication."

6. Communication competence is vital to success and completion of your daily functions. The Self-Assessment chart in Chapter 1 dealing with Communication Competence is a nice evaluation of your strengths and goals. This chart gives you a starting place to

measure your traits and tendencies when expressing yourself in a dispute, conflict, or difference of opinion.

7. Does your diagram indicate that both sending and receiving are simultaneous? How important is feedback? Can you describe the "noise" interfering with the effective sending and receiving of messages? Go back to Chapter 1 in the text and review Figure 1-2.

8. Combining the definition of dyadic communication found in Chapter 1 by Photo 1-5 and then combining the Calvin & Hobbes cartoon regarding self-monitoring; describe how you/why you decided to shape your behavior.

Chapter 2: Answers to Review Questions

Your answers should include the following points:

1. Review the beginning of this chapter and the discussion of "Communication and the Self." Who are you? Make this personal. Identify what affects your self-concept.

2. The definition of self-concept, as described in Chapter 2, reflects how we see our self and our interpretation of how others perceive us. Common characteristics usually cited begin with (but in no way are limited to) age, gender, ethnicity, regional identification, height, weight, religion, and physical attributes.

3. Expectations and assumptions frequently skew the outcome ahead of time. Look at the material covered in Figure 2-1 of this chapter.

4. Review the "Common Perceptual Tendencies" identified in Chapter 2.

5. "Empathy, Perception, and Communication" in Chapter 2 explains the process of empathy application.

6. Refer to the explanations in Chapter 2 that deal with "Characteristics of Identity Management."

7. See the element of Chapter 2 pertaining to "Identity Management in Mediated Communication."

8. The instant reaction tends to be to answer "yes," but there are sensitive and ethical challenges to identity management and honesty. Weigh carefully the judicial balance of how far is too far, how honest is too honest.

Chapter 3: Answers to Review Questions

Your answers should include the following points:

1. Culture and coculture influence everyone's methods of communication. Cultures and cocultures mingle in the classroom, grocery store, entertainment field, and employment choices. Answers will vary, but the first six pages of this chapter should clarify your answer.

2. The meanings of phrases using the same language but with various connotations, the interpretation of nonverbal signals, the frequency or lack thereof of vocal intonations, even the concept of self-centeredness or being a "team player." What you are used to is correct and acceptable; what is different is unsettling and suspicious. There are daily examples of this you should be able to enumerate.

3. Stereotypical thinking and preconceived assumptions often blur the distinction between actual cultural differences and overgeneralizations. A native of Alabama and a working-class resident of New Jersey; a native Texan and an immigrant from India; a teenager from California and a senior citizen from Idaho . . . do you stereotype and overgeneralize? Check the section of this chapter dealing with "Cultural Values and Norms."

4. Compare and contrast individuals in the same age group, with shared ethnicity, identical education, and fairly uniform socioeconomic status with the communication traits of a vastly dissimilar group. What norms, traits, values, and concepts are different? Which group does it "right"? Take the Intercultural Sensitivity Self-Assessment in this chapter.

5. Codes, verbal and nonverbal, and how they are used in cultures vary depending on many influences. You should have an appreciation of the challenges that arise with people from different cultures/cocultures seeking to communicate. Examine the section of this chapter that addresses "Codes and Culture."

6. How open-minded are you? How sensitive are you to other cultures? Take the Intercultural Sensitivity Self-Assessment. Be honest in your answers. Could you improve

your intercultural communication competence? Cite specific examples of what you can do regarding the cultures/cocultures around you in your daily life.

7.   While interacting successfully with strangers calls for the same basic ingredients of general communication competence outlined in Chapter 1, this chapter highlights unique elements for "Developing Intercultural Communication Competence."

8.   Descriptions and examples may vary but they should be in line with Table 3-2 of this chapter.

Chapter 4: Answers to Review Questions

Your answers should include the following points:

1.   The rules of language come with challenges. When there are rules, there are exceptions. Still, the early part of Chapter 4 identifies the rules and gives multiple examples of their applications.

2.   See the examples cited in the text regarding names, credibility, status, sexism, and racism.

3.   Besides shaping the way we view our self and indicating inner thoughts, sometimes unconsciously, the way we use language causes others to form opinions about us. The emotion or power behind our words, the connection with our home or workplace, our likes and dislikes, and our willingness to accept responsibility is an everyday indicator of who we are. Table 4-1 in this chapter and examples from the text that follows explain this in greater detail.

4.   While cultural and cocultural differences do exist, causing statements to be misunderstood, too often the sender is either not precise enough or is deliberately vague. Review the section in Chapter 4 dealing with "Troublesome Language."

5.   The four linguistic acrobatic tricks used to accept and/or reject responsibility are detailed in Chapter 4.

6.   Cartoon 4-6 in Chapter 4 highlights the challenges of "he said/she heard" and "she said/he heard."

7.   There is no right or wrong on the Self-Assessment rubric. It is designed to enlighten and educate.

Chapter 5: Answers to Review Questions

Your answers should include the following points:

1.   While it must be established early that listening and hearing are not the same thing, it is also import to clarify, with examples, the stages of listening as opposed to hearing. This should also include the contrast between mindful versus mindless listening.

2.   It seems apparent that listening ability declines with age. Adults need to be aware of the challenges, some of which are their own fault, hampering effective listening. Examples should include the faulty listening behaviors and personal experiences. This section of Chapter 5 highlights and underlines the faulty listening behaviors with succinct explanations.

3.   Care should be taken to separate the faulty listening behaviors from the reasons for poor listening. The first are conscious obstacles dealing with mindset and attitude; the latter often are unconscious attributes requiring more self-awareness strategies of the process taking place. Review the @Work Box on multitasking in this chapter and follow up with the many reasons for poor listening.

4.   This is designed to help discover listening tendencies. There is no right or wrong; it simply reflects your experiences and goals.

5.   Where the advantages of task-oriented listening assist in organization and efficiency, some people are too preoccupied to be aware of the process. Using the categories from the Self-Assessment chart on listening styles that apply to task-oriented listening can be a way to show the benefits and advantages of this approach.

6.   Emotional connections are easier for extroverts who are attentive and friendly. It can, however, get the listener too involved. The "Ethical Challenges of Relational Listening" section in this chapter underlines some of the drawbacks.

7. "We have an affirmative responsibility to hear the argument before we disagree." To do that we must listen before evaluating, separate the message from the speaker, and search for value.

8. Investigating the accuracy, validity, competence, evidence, and possible emotional involvement of the message itself has merit. The "Critical Listening" section in Chapter 5 offers guidelines for performing this task.

9. The goal of supportive listening is to help the sender, not the receiver. The listener must help and assist with empathy. The types of support enumerated in the "Supportive Listening" section of this chapter all come with advantages and disadvantages.

Chapter 6: Answers to Review Questions

Your answers should include the following points:

1.   The communicative value of nonverbal communication guarantees that you cannot "not" communicate. While open to interpretation, nonverbal communication contributes to identity management and social interaction. Using examples from Table 6-2 to clarify the differences between verbal and nonverbal communication should help make this decipherable.

2.   This answer should include differences in quantity and degree of gestures, use of space and physicality, eye contact, and use of tone and vocal directness or lack thereof.

3.   Prompts such as "Finish this sentence: Big boys don't _____" and "What exactly does it mean to "act like a lady?" could encourage thought-provoking insights. It would be interesting to compare "old-school" stereotypes with the reality of today. When did men stop standing up when a woman entered the room? Do men still open doors and why do some women resent it? This could create interesting dialogue in the classroom.

4.   Look at the insert box on "Understanding Communication Technology" in this chapter. The answers should include emoticons, asterisks, changes in font and print type, abbreviations, capitalization, and multiple methods of emphasis.

5.   The astute observer of self-monitoring will note a contrast in vocal tone and expressions, body language, tone of voice, posture, clothing, appearance, and the use of distance. The realization of territorial power and status and the influence of environment are two other markedly different areas between a party and a job interview.

6.   Does punctuality matter? When? Where? Is it vital to "be on time" or will you "get there when I get there"? Do you use time as an indicator of interest or boredom, respect or rudeness, when responding to messages? A query concerning the Justin Bieber example given in this chapter should prompt engaged classroom discussion.

Chapter 7: Answers to Review Questions

Your answers should include the following points:

1. These factors should include the characteristics of appearance, similarity, complementarity, reciprocal attraction, competence, disclosure, proximity, and rewards, as explained in the first ten pages of this chapter.

2. Figure 7-1 in this chapter clearly designates these stages.

3. See Figure 7-2 of this chapter and the photo on page 214.

4. See the Chapter 7 component "Strategies for Managing Dialectical Tensions."

5. Messages that focus on the subject being discussed

6. Affinity, respect, immediacy, and control

7. Messages that refer to other messages. Examples could include sarcasm, hints, and messages with more than one meaning.

8. See the section of Chapter 7 that discusses "Dimensions of Intimacy."

9. There are seven total, all identified under "Characteristics of Effective Self-Disclosure" in Chapter 7.

10. While answers will vary, the definition of and justification for altruistic lies should be included.

Chapter 8: Answers to Review Questions

Your answers should include the following points:

1. The emotional tone of a relationship

2. The introductory paragraphs of Chapter 8 can help clarify the analogy between weather conditions and relationships. Longer life, better sleep, well-informed intelligence, and an active engaged lifestyle versus the exact opposite—if given the choice, one shines brighter than the other.

3. Confirming messages involve positive responses and disconfirming ones deny, reject, omit, ignore, insult, and neglect the other party involved.

4. An expressed struggle between at least two interdependent parties who perceive incompatible goals, scarce resources, and interference from the other parties in achieving their goals.

5. Nonassertion, direct aggression, passive aggression, indirect communication, and assertion. See Table 8-3 of Chapter 8.

6. Review the component of this chapter "Gender and Conflict Style."

7. See the section "Cultural Influences on Conflict" in this chapter.

8. Table 8-4 of Chapter 8 explains the alternatives and addresses the benefits of compromise.

Chapter 9: Answers to Review Questions

Your answers should include the following points:

1.   See the beginning of this chapter for the definition of a group or team and their distinct characteristics.

2.   The section "Goals of Groups and Their Members" in Chapter 9 discusses group and personal motives.

3.   Rules are the hard-and-fast stipulated guidelines. Norms are the "understood" and unspoken standards of the way things are done.

4.   See Figure 9-1 and Figure 9-2 in Chapter 9.

5.   Formal roles will have titles: Coach, President, Manager, Chair, Supervisor, etc.

6.   Definitions of the communication style of authoritarian, democratic, laissez-faire, and situational leaders are given right after the Self-Assessment of Your Leadership Approach in Chapter 9.

7.   Details are given following the Self-Assessment on How Good a Follower Are You in Chapter 9.

8.   Examples will vary. Legitimate = a title or position; expert = competence and knowledge; connection = networking abilities and contacts; reward = the granting or promise of consequences; coercive = threats, intimidation, punishment; referent= charisma.

Chapter 10: Answers to Review Questions

Your answers should include the following points:

1. The section on "Advantages of Group Problem Solving" at the beginning of Chapter 10 identifies resources, accuracy, commitment, and diversity as things a group possesses that are not available to an individual.

2. Immediately after the "Understanding Diversity" box in Chapter 10, reasons are given for when to use groups to solve problems.

3. The degree to which members feel connected with and committed to their group is reinforced by the elements cited in the "Building Cohesiveness" section of Chapter 10.

4. High-quality solutions come about only with cooperation and communication within the group. Breakout groups report back to a larger body. Problem census works for encouraging participation but protecting anonymity. Focus groups are aimed at a problem but are seldom asked to reach a decision.

5. See Table 10-1 in Chapter 10 and the explanations of these formats in the text thereafter.

6. Review the section of Chapter 10 titled "A Structured Problem-Solving Approach."

7. From "voting" to "commanding" each option has benefits and each has drawbacks. The most effective depends on the circumstances, and this can change depending on the situation.

8. The cartoon on page 318 of Chapter 10 has a point. To overcome this pitfall, members should follow up on suggestions made in the section of the chapter that deals with unequal participation.

Chapter 11: Answers to Review Questions

Your answers should include the following points:

1. Choosing a topic, determining your purpose, and finding information

2. Review the Chapter 11 guidelines for writing an effective purpose statement and examine the Less Effective and More Effective examples listed.

3. Review "The Listener: Audience Analysis" in Chapter 11. Your answer should include cultural diversity, gender, age, group membership, attitudes, beliefs, values, and number of people listening.

4. Time, place, and audience expectations

5. Credibility, objectivity, currency

6. A library catalog, reference works, periodicals, non-print materials such as films, videos, recordings, pictures, physical objects, interviews, and survey research

7. Practice. Practice again. Practice out loud. Practice some more. Be prepared for all contingencies and then practice again.

8. Chapter 11 covers this in the section "Sources of Debilitative Communication Apprehension."

9. Extemporaneous. Impromptu speeches are unplanned and unpracticed. Manuscript speeches take away spontaneity and tend to result in monotone delivery with no eye contact or gestures. Memorized speeches put a lot of pressure on recall, and that usually means talking too fast and glancing at the ceiling periodically.

Chapter 12: Answers to Review Questions

Your answers should include the following points:

1. The working outline helps organize your thoughts, it maps out the progression of the speech from point to point, and it gives you a start to rework and redraft as the final product takes shape.

2. A formal outline can be displayed as a visual aid, can be distributed as a handout, can serve as a record for reviewing, and can be helpful in analyzing the presentation.

3. Review the section in Chapter 12 "Organizing Your Outline Into Logical Patterns."

4. Capture attention, preview the subject, set the mood and tone, and demonstrate the importance of the topic

5. Many approaches can be used to get the attention of the audience. See "Checklist: Capturing Audience Attention" in Chapter 12.

6. Be well prepared, appear confident, and tell your audience about your personal experience with the topic.

7. Restate thesis, review main points, and provide a memorable ending.

8. Review "Checklist: Effective Conclusions" in Chapter 12.

9. See the section "Supporting Material" in Chapter 12.

10. See "Types of Supporting Material" in Chapter 12.

Chapter 13: Answers to Review Questions

Your answers should include the following points:

1. Address the needs of the listener, engage and involve the audience, make it easy to listen to, and employ interesting and stimulating supporting material.

2. Limit the amount of information you present, use familiar material to increase understanding of the unfamiliar, use simple to build to complex.

3. See "Checklist: Techniques of Informative Speaking" in Chapter 13.

4. Personalize the speech, use audience participation or volunteers, have a Q & A session not just at the end of the speech but during it.

5. There is a wide variety of choices for visual aids. The rules relate to their simplicity, size, attractiveness, appropriateness, and reliability.

6. Pros = focuses audience attention, makes logical structure transparent, and gives a visual source for vocal words. Cons = trivializes important information, encourages oversimplification, and discourages interaction with lack of speaker eye contact and movement.

7. Informative speeches tend to be noncontroversial and non-confrontational. Informative speeches add knowledge without opinion.

8. The first is repetition— I repeat, repetition. The second is signposts.

Chapter 14: Answers to Review Questions

Your answers should include the following points:

1.   Convincing

2.   Reinforce, sometimes strengthen, or at least begin the shift of attitudes.

3.   Actuating

4.   Adoption or discontinuance

`5.   See Table 14-1 of Chapter 14 for a lengthy list of unethical communication behaviors.

6.   Believability

7.   Competence, character, charisma

8.   Review the section of Chapter 14 titled "Adapting to the Audience."

9.   These errors in logic are listed with Latin as well as English labels in the section of Chapter 14 dealing with how to avoid fallacies.

10.   Indirect

11.   Attention, need, satisfaction, visualization, call for action

12. Force, intimidation, threat, blackmail, arm-twisting, brow-beating, bullying, and not allowing the listener to have a choice

Appendix C: Thinking Outside the Box Questions

Chapter 1: Answers to Thinking Outside the Box

1. Answers will vary. Journal entries usually indicate frustration and stress. There is more than one study detailing a separation anxiety referred to as Internet Addiction Disorder, but the purpose of this exercise is not to validate that syndrome. Asking someone to stop doing something that has become such an integral element of his or her life highlights the material in the text: total abstinence is a shock to the system. Appreciating and understanding the value of face-to-face and mediated communication in today's society is the aim of this exercise. For guidance review Table 1-1 in Chapter 1.

2. Chapter One, Table 1-1, comes into play here once again. This combined with the chart of the Accelerating Pace of Communication Technology highlights the value and priorities assigned to communication by today's consumers of the medium.

3. Movies such as "Eat, Pray, Love," "Up in the Air," and "Cast Away" all employ the many types of communication defined in Chapter 1. There is a link to relevant websites, study aids, and examples pertaining to communication types at www.oup.com/us/adler.

4. Decisions regarding effective communication can be directly connected to experience and age. Review the chart of the Accelerating Pace of Communication Technology and then check out Chapter 1's explanation of "Communicating Effectively with Social Media." Table 1-2 guides a competent communicator in Choosing a Communication Channel.

Chapter 2: Answers to Thinking Outside the Box

1. A self-analysis presents the challenge of choosing between circumspect language and bluntness. Review Chapter 2's section dealing with honesty.

2. For both Precious and Temple there were many common perceptual tendencies used as barriers in their dealings with others. The character of Dominic in "Fast and Furious" also has expectations to fulfill based on what others think of him. Not the very different identity perpetuated due to perceptions.

3. When are you the most in line with your perceived self? When are you the most honest? Do you ever alter your presenting self? Why? When do "you" cross the line? These are points to ponder for future communication.

4. Establishing identity and defending that self-concept is a tendency of most groups. New members, in this case visitors and guests to the family gathering, are expected to adapt to norms and expectations. Compare and contrast your experiences when you are the "new person" to the experiences when you bring an outsider to your in-group.

Chapter 3: Answers to Thinking Outside the Box

1. Do you have cultural diversity in your modern family? Identify the cultures, cocultures, and disparities in "sameness" within your family.

2. How far do you have to search to be out of your comfort zone? How long does it take to get acclimated to the patterns of communication not normal for your culture/coculture? Note the differences.

3. Answers will vary but every place of employment has a "culture." Disney calls tourists "guests" and employees "cast members." A bookstore uses language of "ISBN's" and "remainders." Academics talk about "load" differently than a dealer at a sporting goods store. Texas A & M has a different coculture than Petsmart.

4. Every generation lays claim to superior cultural insight and a specific jargon for communicating. Then the next generation supplants the old with its version . . . only to be moved aside by the next, etc. Still, it is a bit jarring for some to discover that the more things change the more they stay the same.

Chapter 4: Answers to Thinking Outside the Box

1. Honesty comes with a coating of bluntness that can wound and cause relationship harm. Review the section of Chapter 4 that deals with equivocation.

3. Offensive words and phrases are rampant in the paragraph.

Did you hear what happened to me at the <u>choke and puke</u> diner? This <u>sawed-off old witch</u> with <u>spikey hair sticking up like cactus bristles</u> pointed her <u>gnarled knobby twisted knuckles</u> at me and, in a <u>screeching voice that sounded like rusty hinges,</u> said I was <u>drunk</u>. Can you believe that? Then she started <u>hacking and coughing like a cat with a hairball</u>. Next thing I knew these two <u>rent-a-cops</u> came up to me—one <u>looked like he had been around since Moses came down off the mountain</u> and the other was a <u>snot-nosed new hire</u>—and they <u>barked</u> at me to haul my <u>bony hind-end</u> out of there. I didn't want to eat in that <u>roach coach</u> anyway, so I <u>gave them the finger</u> and left.

Get three or four students together to come up with choices and possibilities, always remembering to "soften" the offensive word or phrase.

3. Who is involved? In what circumstances does the behavior occur? What behaviors are involved?

Chapter 5: Answers to Thinking Outside the Box

1. The person reciting the words should complement each with certain actions. BEGIN is a clear beginning statement. When saying WALK, walk. When saying RUN, shout it and run. Stand still and do not make eye contact when saying STUDY. Turn your back on the listeners for HORSEFEATHERS. Repeat REPEAT four times. Wave your arms frantically for CORN. Smile when you say EASY. Write LISTEN on the board as you say it. Say MANEUVER quickly and softly. Shake your head when saying COAT. Rush MASTICATION. Announce NUMBER THIRTEEN IS THE NUMBER THIRTEEN. Say SLOW slowly. Cross your arms in finality and announce STOP. The outcome is predictable: a large majority of listeners get BEGIN, WALK, and RUN because they were in the beginning and movement matched words. STUDY and HORSEFEATHERS have listeners drop off because listening was discouraged. REPEAT will be retained because it was repeated. CORN doesn't make sense and EASY seems exactly too easy. Nearly everyone will get LISTEN because there was a visual aid, but there will be a drastic drop-off for MANEUVER and COAT as everyone is still focused on the visual aid. MASTICATION is a complicated word many do not know and thus will not get. THIRTEEN has a mental connection to the placement, and listeners usually return in mass numbers when they know the listening is concluding, so SLOW and STOP will have large results.

2. Choose a sentence that is complicated and unfamiliar. Try this one: "A collection of dwarves, I think there were eight, had spinach for lunch on Wednesday and rode their bicycles home from work yesterday." Insist that the rumor-spreaders whisper, and while the message is being transferred, the "coordinator" should keep up a steady patter of conversation, instructions, and anecdotes. At the conclusion remind everyone of the challenges of attending, understanding, responding, and remembering and overcoming noise. The end result, by the way, is always quite creative and very inaccurate.

3. While answers will vary, the journal should be filled with situations and examples of the myriad reasons for poor listening, including some from the journal keeper.

Chapter 6: Answers to Thinking Outside the Box

1.   Posture, gestures, eye contact, facial expressions, clothing, touch, even vocalizations (but not actual words) can substitute quite adequately for verbal communication in many situations. At first the experiment might appear to be an acting lesson in pantomime, but if the nonverbal-only user is subtle and yet earnest, many times the complete hour passes and no one else will notice the change. The sender will experience more frustration than the receiver.

2.   Standing "too close" in an elevator, invading personal and even intimate space while asking for directions, and being just slightly too far away for dyadic interaction can be unsettling and could cause involuntary reactions and noticeable nonverbal feedback.

3.   Emoticons, italics, asterisks, capitalizations, altering font or size, spacing, and/or hash-tag commentary alters the meaning of the identical words. The reciprocation should be quite interesting.

Chapter 7: Answers to Thinking Outside the Box

1. While some respondents will still have the same friend, they should recognize that the relationship has gone through varying stages, both coming together and coming apart. Others will no longer have a relationship with the third-grade friend and will have an explanation for the terminating stage.

2. Developing insight into personal motives and intimacy styles can be very enlightening in future interpersonal relationships. The self-assessment in Chapter 7 could also be used by couples to establish relational understanding.

3. Since the majority of our communication is relatively impersonal, altering that relationship to an interpersonal one involves time, commitment, and energy. Employing the tools of affinity, respect, immediacy, and control could sway the balance between impersonal and interpersonal.

4. Sharing emotional and intellectual intimacy solidifies interpersonal relationships. Preliminary reactions could result in consternation, frustration, irritation, and aggravation. The revelation that the odd behavior was a "classroom experiment" should prompt appreciation and investigation into constructive communication (we hope!).

Chapter 8: Answers to Thinking Outside the Box

1. While forming a diagnosis with just four questions seems simplistic, the Self-Assessment evaluation in Chapter 8 gives the test-taker an insight into setting the climate and responding with the best chance for success.

2. The example highlights confirming messages and shows the results of aggression as opposed to assertion. Constructive differences can be discussed without every conflict scaling up into a funnel cloud of hurt, anger, and frustration.

3. Evaluative language occurs often in the academic field: professors and students conversing, students chiding other students, parents and students, young people talking to older people, employers talking to employees. While correcting the sender might result in an escalatory spiral, the rewritten alternatives could heighten awareness and behavioral adjustments in the observer.

Chapter 9: Answers to Thinking Outside the Box

1. Honest self-evaluation helps group participants recognize their attributes and their weaknesses. Some people strive for leadership roles and then are flummoxed and frustrated; some work best in support and cooperation. These two self-assessments assist in clarifying the difference.

2. We belong to many more groups or teams than we initially think. The rules are evident and obvious. The education and discovery process of how one "learns" the norms usually involves an orientation from a mentor, advisor, guide, or companion.

3. Is there a personality type willing to lead? Is one person more effective at leading than another? Why? Are some participants more willing to follow and more reluctant to lead? Are some followers more engaged than others? Why? An impromptu group suddenly assigned a simple task will still develop predictable patterns of leaders and followers.

Chapter 10: Answers to Thinking Outside the Box

1.   Many teams have the mindset "This is the way it has always been." Reviewing and implementing effective communication by improving cohesiveness and involving the dysfunctional members could raise the self-assessment score much higher.

2.   Problem-solving situations exist all around us. It can be valuable to step back and watch the process without a vested interest or hidden agenda. Seeing the repercussions of the decision instills awareness of the burden of leadership and responsibility.

3.   The stress and tension of moving plus the juxtaposition of a friend now being the decision-maker, or vice versa, can cause relational breakdowns in cohesiveness and achieving the goal. Which way to tilt the couch going out the door? What to load first; what to unload last? Who calls for breaks and rest periods? Are there too many leaders and not enough followers? What if the leader is at the old location and a decision must be made at the new location? When the task is completed, is the shared experience one that furthers or fractures cohesiveness?

Chapter 11: Answers to Thinking Outside the Box

1. Without knowing the audience ahead of time, the success or failure of such a speech depends a great deal on making the purpose clear and specific. Another benefit of preparing an elevator speech is that you will get used to bragging about yourself, overcoming the tendency to find fault and be your own worst critic.

2. Speakers who do not encourage audience engagement by using visual and vocal aspects of delivery will most likely lose their audience and will definitely not imprint the information for response.

3. Whom am I talking to: teachers, students, or parents? What is the audience expecting? How many people will be there? When am I speaking? For how long? Where? What time of day? What do they know about checkers now? Is someone speaking before me or after me? How should I dress? The point to all this is to know as much about the audience and expectations as possible before putting your speech together.

Chapter 12: Answers to Thinking Outside the Box

1. The idea is to appreciate the thought put into organizing and structuring a speech. The outline pattern, whichever one is preferred, also aids in instilling confidence in knowledge of the subject and ease of discussing it in a conversational delivery without writing the speech out word for word.

2. Answers will vary but the statements should all capture the audience's attention, set the mood and tone, preview main points, and demonstrate the importance of the topic.

3. Examples are many, unfortunately, in books, movies, songs, and speeches. The four mistakes are: don't end abruptly, don't ramble, don't introduce new points, and don't apologize.

Chapter 13: Answers to Thinking Outside the Box

1. Since there is a plethora of information bombarding us constantly, the skill of turning information into knowledge is one that requires focus and effort. A competent informative speaker uses all the techniques recommended in Chapter 13 plus the knowledge acquired from previous chapters in this text to create information hunger, make it personal, utilize the visual and vocal aspects of delivery, and help the audience "get it" in a non-intrusive, non-aggressive manner.

2. Examples will vary, but using "this happened to me" always intrigues the listener. The speaker can have the listener stand in a certain place or contribute to the presentation by moving or responding, by "acting out" particular components of the speech, or by giving feedback. Doing a "check-back"—asking quick yes-or-no questions and waiting for the response ("Are you with me to this point?" "Bet you see what is coming next." " You know what she said?")—can pull the listener into the presentation as an engaged, involved participant.

3. Graphs, charts, and statistics put most audience members to sleep. Visuals that are too hard to see, too complicated, overly explained, or too static shut down the information processes in listeners. A darkened room and a monotone voice take us back to nap time in kindergarten. No enthusiasm on the part of the speaker, no movement or complementary gestures, and dull PowerPoint or Prezi presentations turn audience members into zombies. The speaker should never give the listener time to think, "I'm bored."

Chapter 14: Answers to Thinking Outside the Box

1. While some commercials are in-your-face direct, others are more subtle. Some commercials want instant action the minute they cease, while others offer an option of thinking about their sales pitch. Celebrities add their charisma to products when they are not experts. Some commercials criticize the opposing messenger and ignore the opposing message. Then there are those making outrageous claims, albeit in jest, that mock or insult objections. Of course there are the commercials practically screaming ultimatums. Some commercials, such as new luxury cars or alcoholic beverages, insinuate that if you use their product you will be good-looking, sophisticated, popular, and mysterious. Other commercials insist you adhere to their campaign because it is the popular thing to do. It will not take long to identify all the logical fallacies mentioned in the text.

2. Without point-blank asking if the audience member is for something or against it, the researcher needs to generate questions that quantify values, beliefs, and attitudes that are similar to the topic about to be presented. The questions need to assist the speaker in determining common ground shared by speaker and audience. The answers should prepare the speaker for the response to be faced; this, in turn, determines whether to use the direct or indirect technique.

3. Persuasion is incremental. It is rare for someone to make a sudden, instantaneous, drastic change from an anchor opinion to the other end of the diagram. Instead, it takes time; it takes input from peers, family, and the media; and it requires experience and education and tiny gradual movements. Reflecting on personal experiences should help the speaker preparing for a speech today to be realistic and reasonable in the persuasive call for action.

4. While the answers will vary, odds are that politicians and celebrities will be on both lists. Character is a personal judgment quality often linked with charisma. People we like get more leeway than people we do not like. Competence is measureable but restricted by the respondent's level of expertise. To a third-grader a sixth-grader is a competent scholar, but to a high-school senior the sixth grader is ignorant and naïve. The measure is relative based on the skill or knowledge of the beholder.

NOTES

NOTES